Diane M. Gayeski, Ph.D., is a partner in OmniCom Associates, specializing in interactive media design and production. She is also an associate professor of corporate/organizational media at Ithaca College and the author of *Corporate and Instructional Video: Design and Production* (Prentice-Hall, 1983).

David V. Williams, Ph.D., is a partner in OmniCom Associates, a firm specializing in new informational/instructional media strategies, where he has developed systems for interactive communications and testing for major companies worldwide. He is also an associate professor of psychology at Ithaca College in Ithaca, New York.

Diane Gayeski
David Williams

INTERACTIVE MEDIA

A SPECTRUM BOOK

Prentice-Hall, Inc., Englewood Cliffs, New Jersey 07632

Library of Congress Cataloging in Publication Data

Gayeski, Diane M., (Date)
  Interactive media.

  "A Spectrum Book."
  Includes index.
    1. Interactive computer systems.   2. Videotex
(Data transmission system)   I. Williams, David V.
II. Title.
QA76.9.I58G39 1984   001.64   84-17847
ISBN 0-13-469289-6
ISBN 0-13-469131-8 (pbk.)

10 9 8 7 6 5 4 3 2 1

ISBN 0-13-469289-6

ISBN 0-13-469131-8 {PBK.}

Editorial/production supervision: Joe O'Donnell Jr.
Cover design: Hal Siegel
Cover photo: Michel Tcherevkoff
Manufacturing buyer: Gary Orso

Prentice-Hall International, Inc., *London*
Prentice-Hall of Australia Pty. Limited, *Sydney*
Prentice-Hall Canada Inc., *Toronto*
Prentice-Hall of India Private Limited, *New Delhi*
Prentice-Hall of Japan, Inc., *Tokyo*
Prentice-Hall of Southeast Asia Pte. Ltd., *Singapore*
Whitehall Books Limited, *Wellington, New Zealand*
Editoria Prentice-Hall do Brasil Ltda., *Rio de Janeiro*
Prentice-Hall Hispanoamericana, S.A., *Mexico*

CONTENTS

ACKNOWLEDGMENTS

The authors would like to thank the following colleagues who contributed original essays to this book: Douglas P. Brush, Partner, D/J Brush Associates, Cold Spring, NY; Judson Rosebush, President, Digital Effects, Inc., New York, NY; Maria Manhattan, Electronic Artist, New York, NY; Michel Borque, Ph.D., Director, Computer & Biostatistics Center, Clinical Research Institute of Montréal, Montréal, Canada; Robert Perreault, M.D., Clinical Research Institute of Mental Health, Montréal, Canada; Donna Demac, Staff Counsel, Office of Communication, United Church of Christ, New York, NY; Carolyn Swift, Ph.D., Manager of Interactive Development & Training, QUBE, Columbus, OH; Lynn Hessinger, Associate, OmniCom Associates, Stamford, CT; Greg Kearsley, Ph.D., Chief Scientist, Courseware, Inc., Alexandria, VA; Robert Oberman, Attorney-at-Law, Omaha, NB; Myra Oberman, Legal Assistant, Omaha, NB; Robert C. Houston, Ph.D., American Airlines Flight Academy, DFW Airport, TX; David Hon, President, IXION, Inc., Seattle, WA; Max Carpenter, Director of Special Projects, Maritime Institute of Technology & Graduate Studies, Linthicum Heights, MD; Carl Frederick, Ph.D., Chief Scientist, Wolfdata, Inc., Chelmsford, MA; Doug Green, Director of Computer Services, Binghamton City Schools, Binghamton, NY; and Stephen Andrade, Systems Trainer, I.R.I.S., Brown University, Providence, RI.

The excerpt on pages 46–47 and the one on page 64 are from *The Future of Videotext: Worldwide Prospects for Home/Office Electronic Information Services,* by Efrem Sigel, with Peter Sommer, Jeffrey Silverstein, Colin McIntyre, and Blaise Downey. Copyright © 1983. Reprinted by permission of Knowledge Industry Publications, Inc., White Plains, N.Y.

The excerpt on page 75 is from "The Electronic Rorschach," D.

CHAPTER ONE

INTRODUCTION

Computers . . . media . . . interaction . . . communication.

It all started with a stick dug in the dirt. Rather than roaming the earth in search of herds and orchards, someone started civilization by making holes in the ground. Into some went seeds, in others, fence posts. Now the herds and orchards could be kept conveniently and predictably right outside the kitchen door. Those holes in the ground were really a form of information. Planting said to the orchard, "Grow here and now," while fence-building gave the herds the message. "Don't wander too far out of reach."

But what "kitchen door?" It had to be built. And whose door was it? It had to be owned within a community. The skills of door-building and door-owning became the hallmark of our species: the use of tools and ideas.

The same stick that created the information structures of furrows and fences was used to trace maps and diagrams of the herds and orchards around the community fire. Those images in the dirt influenced the next day's work in the fields and pastures. The interdependence of tools and ideas are as old as humanity. New tools create new ideas create new tools create new communications create new tools. . . .

The technician explaining the manufacturing robot's terminal input to a trainee is still a person scratching in the dirt around the community fire. The basic nature of the human interaction remains the same, but the setting is certainly different. How did we get from there to here, and where are we all going?

The image of Three Waves that Alvin Toffler (1980) has provided is a useful starting point. The beginning of agriculture (the First Wave) marks the start of civilization—or "city-ification." It initiated the technical skills (such as construction) and social concepts (such as "property rights") that we associate with human society. Sharing space and performing more complex, multiperson tasks over longer periods of time catapulted communication into new importance. Plans, agreements, and disagreements had to be accomplished, because there was a commitment to the place and people that was not a part of nomadic life. Concepts of time, space, self, and others arose. Representations of these ideas through symbols, such as words, dance movements, and ceremonial objects, became the information technology of the time.

The meanings of these symbols were preserved in the "oral tradition"—through human memory. Tool use followed the same pattern. These devices were fairly direct extensions of skilled human movement, the development and use of which were an integral part of ongoing human interaction. If people stopped using a tool or forgot a ritual, these elements would disappear. All technology and communication were, therefore, *interactive.*

Meanwhile, social organization, communication, and the tools of transportation expanded a person's range in time and space so that new concepts and technologies of communication (e.g., writing) were required. This, in turn, made travel possible. The cooperation among the extended families of the tribe gave way to complex relationships among anonymous citizens of a nation whose daily lives were dependent upon a shared belief in its flag and coins. These symbols, along with the written word, began to be removed from the immediate influence of village groups. Of course, tools themselves were becoming more complex, perhaps taking their cue from the specialization in crafts (sometimes amounting to assembly lines). Tools began to be strung together so that movements of one tool could perform a task *and* provide information initiating movement in another tool, becoming a "machine."

While tools require information (skill) for use, machines contain some of that information themselves. Machines, occupational specialization, and social hierarchies are all situations in which the information necessary to complete a task does not lie in a group of cooperating individuals who communicate that knowledge. Information and technology became more linear. While machines had some skill, their power source was usually some kind of muscle, wind, or water. Applying the fire of fossil fuels began the industrial revolution. From the point of view of the relationships between tools, information, and people, there was nothing new in principle, but the scope of centralized industrial society grew into the Second Wave. It brought about interdependence among far-flung individuals as unknown to each other as they were bound together in the communication system of contracts and trade agreements.

The remainder of the machine's information and power is provided by the person, but as more information was placed in the machine, the thought arose: Why not use a machine to process information? The Third Wave was breaking.

The analytical engine of Charles Babbage looks like it had Rube Goldberg as its design consultant, but its importance is that it is a machine that neither uses nor produces raw materials—it just rearranges symbols. There were information tools (like the abbacus), but this was an information machine: a series of tools with information in them to process symbols. It worked with numbers because that communication system has the simplest processing rules.

The development of electricity affected all machines, including information processors. Instead of moving beads on a rod or numbered cogs, electric switches—then magnetic charges—could be used. The first information machines to be called computers were barn-sized collections of vacuum tubes attended by teams of runners to replace the burned-out tubes. Like all machines, the information was part of their structure; each performed only one process upon whatever numbers were fed in. Being able to change that information easily would make the machine more responsive to a particular need, returning some of the skill to the user.

That's exactly the giant step that the programmability of computers brought about. This capability is still developing as programming languages are being written that translate from the symbols and processes people use into the off/on electronic pulses of computer core and back to human-oriented information.

Even the commercially available computers of recent decades were huge, hand-built machines sensitive to temperature, vibration, and humidity. Their location and accessibility was quite limited. Since they also performed only one programmed task at a time, people had to stand in line with their boxes of punched cards. Of course, mistakes only showed up the next day. Thus, the information machine still remained a very linear part of the styles of the Second Wave.

The development of magnetic tape meant that it could sort through the jobs to send in several small ones at once and receive information at human pace, using the computer perhaps for only a few minutes per hour. This ability opened up computer access and developed a style of interchange between human thought, computer use, and programming undreamed of by those used to waiting anxiously in line for their "turnaround."

However, at the end of all the terminals was still a large, expensive, and somewhat temperamental collection of circuits. The Third Wave was lapping at the sandy shore from which the silicon transistor was to come. The same savings in size and price of portable radios, smaller and cheaper to make and run, came to computers. Then came the microchip, an incredibly complicated circuit reproduced by photography, bringing size and price down again. Many of us now take for granted that a typewriter-sized microcomputer more powerful than nearly all the commercial computers of a decade ago can be purchased locally for the price of a used car.

But the personal computer is anything but a miniature mainframe. It is so different in its hardware, software, and applications that it cannot really be understood as a "computer." Many people's concept of microcomputers is left over from the rigid mainframes designed a decade ago (and often still in use). These systems can often only deal in numbers and block letters typed in and out in strict formats. Taking information in and putting it out in batches, many of these number crunchers communicate with us tersely, if at all. They are often convenient scapegoats for human error. Whether based on stereotypes or experience with antiquated hardware or programming styles, the "does not compute" experience is a far cry from many well-designed microcomputer interactions. In addition to size, price, and reliability, micros are easy to program. This led to a wide cross section of non-computer people developing applications and exchanging ideas and programs. The microcomputer was also designed to *communicate* with people in all of their modalities, color, images, sound, speech, and movement, and to reach out beyond itself through interfaces to interrelate human communication and non-computer devices. In fact, its microchips are now the information components of many machines themselves.

TECHNOLOGY AND COMMUNICATION

What does the history of computers have to do with media? These digital wonders have emerged from their traditional data-processing tasks to becoming means for communications. As Nora and Minc (1980) point out, the two worlds of broadcast telecommunications and data processing communications have merged. Now, information transmission will become two-way, and computers will be seen as important communication devices. Our new electronic environment will enable us to communicate much more rapidly, efficiently, vividly, and cheaply than ever before.

> The new electronic environment is a metamorphosis of the conditions under which life on earth has developed. It erases old dimensions of distance and time. It transcends limitations of the physical environment. In this new environment, almost all of humanity can witness the same experiences simultaneously, or an infinite variety of differing ones. The electronic environment is instantaneously changeable. It can directly link more human minds, minds with ideas, and minds with machines than any communications means we have developed in our 36,000-year spoken or 6,000-year written heritage. It is permeating, energizing, stultifying, mesmerizing, trivializing, delighting, and dulling. But it is totally artifactual. We create it and we can control it. (Williams, 1982)

Many questions remain open: How can we best harness the computer's power to enhance our communications? Will computers, in fact, inhibit communication? How will new forms of interactive media change our concepts and precepts? What kinds of skills will be needed for the 21st century "Renaissance" communicator? Many of us, quite adept with the traditional written and spoken word, feel utterly helpless in the face of the new possibilities these electronic/digital systems offer.

Waiting for Gigo*

Some 98 percent of all households have television sets, yet more people are interested in getting personal computers than in getting video cassette or videodisc players.

For most, the decision of what to buy is relatively easy . . . they know nothing about computers and rely on what George Plimpton, Bill

*by Douglas P. Brush.

Cosby or other product spokesmen tell them in the television commercials. They're happy with whatever the machine does since they have no clear idea of what they'll use it for.

Ah . . . but for us high-tech sophisticates it's a different story. We know *what we're doing.* We're used to spending days, weeks and months researching and analyzing video cameras, VTRs, videodiscs, switchers, effects generators and the like to match the needs of our organizations or our clients.

Equipment may change in features and price, but the technology stays pretty much the same from year to year. Hardware bought today will do almost the same job as similar equipment bought two years from now.

Not so with computers. New systems are introduced almost weekly that do things previous models couldn't, even those from the same manufacturer.

As a result, as soon as we make a decision on an Apple, along comes the IBM PC. That looks good until we see the Osborne and KayPro. But they pale next to Lisa, whose mouse is then trapped by Texas Instruments' new Professional Computer. In the meantime, people like Otrona keep packing bits and bytes into ever smaller briefcase-sized packages that can go anywhere.

What to do. What to do.

We feel like the characters in Beckett's Waiting for Godot, *lost in a limbo of unreality and indecision.*

[Scene: An empty office. A desk. A chair. Late afternoon. Byte is sitting on the chair hopelessly trying to stack a pile of papers that slip and slide into a shapeless heap at his feet. Enter Bit.]

Bit: (Despairing) Nothing to be done. Nothing to be done!

Byte: So there you are again. Where have you been?

Bit: Hiding in a ditch.

Byte: Did they beat you again?

Bit: Beat me? Certainly they beat me.

Byte: The same lot as usual?

Bit: The same? I don't know. They all seem alike.

Byte: They can't all be alike. Read their ads. Each is the best. They say so. Each is the only one to do everything. Each is the least expensive. It makes no difference what it costs. (His pile of papers collapses once more).

Bit: What are you doing?

Byte: Processing. What does it look like?

Bit: Processing what?

Byte: (Irritably) Words. Numbers. What difference does it make. Things have to be processed. Every day. You know that! (Feebly) Help me! [Bit slowly walks around the empty office, ends facing the audience.]

Bit: (Bitterly) Charming place. (Pause) Let's go.

Byte: We can't.

Bit: Why not?

Byte: We're waiting for GiGo.

Bit: You're sure it was to be here?

Byte: He said by the desk. Do you see any others?

Bit: He should be here.

Byte: He didn't say for sure he'd come.

Bit: And if he doesn't come?

Byte: We'll come back tomorrow.

Bit: And then the day after tomorrow?

Byte: Possibly.

Bit: You're sure it was today?

Byte: He said today. (Pause) I think. I must have made a note of it. (He frantically searches through the pile of papers.)

Bit: Are we tied?

Byte: How do you mean?

Bit: Down.

Byte: To whom? By whom?

Bit: To GiGo?

Byte: Tied to GiGo? What an idea! (Pause. Looks at the pile of papers. Moves them around with his foot.) No question of it. For the moment.

Bit: His name is GiGo?

Byte: I think so.

Bit: Fancy that.

[A terrible cry, close at hand. Bit and Byte clutch each other, cringing away from the approaching menace. They wait. Enter Systems Manager and Main Frame. SM drives MF by a rope made of magnetic tape passed around his neck. MF carries several heavy bags and boxes. SM carries a whip.]

SM: (Cracks whip.) Enter! (Stops short at sight of Bit and Byte. Magnetic tape rope tautens. SM jerks at it violently.) Back! (MF staggers and falls, dropping bags and boxes. Printouts scatter at Bit's and Byte's feet. Bit takes a step towards MF. Byte holds his sleeve.)

Bit: Let me go!

Byte: Stay where you are!

SM: Be careful! He's wicked. (Pause. Ominously.) With *users*!

Bit: (Undertone.) Is that him?

Byte: Who?

Bit: (Trying to remember the name.) Er. . . your friend. . .

Byte: GiGo?

Bit: Yes.

SM: I present myself. Systems Manager.

Byte: (To Bit) Not at all!

Bit: (Timidly to SM) You're not Mr. GiGo, sir?

SM: (Terrifying voice) I am Systems Manager! (Silence) Does that name mean *nothing* to you?

Bit: Systems. . .no. . .I'm afraid I. . .I don't seem to. . .

Byte: We're not from DP, sir.

SM: But I see you are processors none the less. (Peers at them through the hole in a large reel of computer tape he is carrying.) As far as one can see, that is. (Bursts into enormous laugh) The same species as I!

Bit: Well you see. . .

SM: (Peremptory) You took *me* for GiGo?

Byte: Oh no, sir, not for an instant, sir.

Bit: True, we don't know him very well.

SM: So you are waiting for him? Here? In *my* area?

Bit: We didn't intend any harm.

Byte: We meant well. It's just. . .well. . .you see we have all this processing to do.

Bit: And we thought. . .well, we hoped. . . that is. . .

Byte: Prayed, as it were. . .

Bit: That Mr. GiGo would help us, sir.

SM: (With magnanimous gesture.) Let's say no more about it. (He jerks the tape rope.) Up pig! (Pause) Every time he crashes he loses his memory. (Jerks the rope.) Up, hog! (MF staggers to his feet and begins packing printouts into the boxes and bags.) Gentlemen, I am happy to have met you. Would you like to see him dance, recite, do vast sums in his head?

Bit: No need to trouble you, sir.

Byte: (Silences Bit with a warning glance.) That would indeed be a pleasure, sir. (Looks at Bit and nods toward the pile of papers.)

SM: (To MF) Boot up, pig! Dance. . .process. . .recite! (Jerks tape rope. MF begins to dance and recite. SM takes a chicken leg from his pocket and begins to eat it. He waves the bone in time with MF's dance and recitation.) How do you find me? (Bit and Byte look at him blankly.) Good? Fair? Middling? Poor? Positively bad?

Bit: Oh very good, very very good.

Byte: Yes indeed. very very good. (Eyes stack of papers apprehensively.)

SM: Bless you, gentlemen, bless you! (Pause) I have such need of encouragement! (Jerks tape rope.) Faster, pig, faster! (MF speeds up his dance and recitation, breathing heavily with eyes bulging.)

Bit: (To Byte) It's a scandal!

SM: What?

Byte: To treat a creature. . .(gestures towards MF) like that. It's a scandal!

SM: (Continues to gnaw chicken leg while MF performs. He throws the bone to the ground.) Stop, pig! (To Bit and Byte.) I must be getting on. Thank you for your society. (Bit looks longingly at the bone on the ground. SM makes as if to go.)

Bit: Please, sir. The bone. Will you be wanting it?

SM: It's yours. (Pause) Good luck with your processing. Sorry I can be of no further help to you. (To MF) Ready pig! Forward! (They exit.)

Bit: (Picks up the bone and puts it in his pocket.) That passed the time.

Byte: It would have passed in any case.

Bit: Yes, but not so rapidly. (Pause) What do we do now?

Byte: We wait.

Bit: For GiGo?

Byte: Yes.

[Enter boy timidly. He carries a small personal computer.]

Boy: Mr. Byte?

Byte: What do you want?

Boy: Mr. GiGo . . .

Byte: (Angry) Speak!

Boy: (All in a rush) Mr. GiGo told me to tell you he won't come today but surely tomorrow.

Bit: Is that all?

Boy: Yes, sir.
(Silence)

Byte: You work for Mr. GiGo?

Boy: Yes, sir.

Byte: What do you do?

Boy: I mind the computers, sir.

Bit: Does he beat you?

Boy: No sir, not me. He beats my brother, sir.

Bit: He must be fond of you.
(Silence)

Byte: You may go. Tell Mr. GiGo. . . tell him you saw us. (Pause) You did see us, didn't you?

Boy: Yes, sir! (He turns and exits running.) (Silence. Bit sits in the chair. Byte kicks at the pile of papers.)

Bit: Where shall we go?

Byte: Not far.

Bit: Let's go far away from here.

Byte: We can't. We have to come back tomorrow.

Bit: What for?

Byte: To wait for GiGo.

Bit: And if he comes?

Byte: We'll be saved.
(Silence)

Bit: Well? Shall we go?
(Pause)

Byte: Yes, let's go. (They do not move.)

The End

The new interactive media technologies may baffle us, yet most of us are intrigued with the possibilities they offer. "Especially in a democratic society, hardly anyone will oppose more information and or restrictions on the rest of the apparatus of the information environment" (Dizard, 1982). New computer-based technologies are having a tremendous impact on traditional media: computer animation races across movie theatre screens, computer graphics on magazine covers, interactive video discs on dusty, 1978-model TV monitors in corporate training rooms, and video games in old pool halls. However, the technologies are opening *new* channels for communication as well.

The "de-massification" of media is happening in two ways: (1) new technology is enabling more of us to "own" communications channels once restricted to a few large publishers or broadcasters; (2) media are now capable of tailoring themselves to individual users, so that one "program" creates different experiences for different people. Rather than the homogeneous mass communications and mass culture of the Industrial Revolution, the new interactive media foster diversity. "The media giants, particularly the TV networks, now face a technological revolution in electronic communications whose outcome will be a proliferation of local programming and special interest channels: narrowcasting in place of broadcasting. These developments in technology and the media arrive in the wake of the myth of America as a melting pot. Ethnic identity, racial pride, gender consciousness and generational awareness are carving our society into an ever finer grid of groupings" (Hawken, et al., 1982). And so, for all of us involved in communications (as creators or users), the new computer and interactive technologies pose some interesting challenges.

This book is not about computers, nor about technology per se. It explores the roles of the new interactive media—computer graphics and animation, teletex, computer-assisted instruction, interactive video, simulations, and intelligent systems. By discussing what each technology is, how it is used to create and disseminate messages, and what its implications are, we hope to provide a framework for understanding the "new wave" of media and communication paradigms. By interacting with these information machines, they become tools for human communication—welcome at our fireside.

REFERENCES

Dizard, W., *The Coming Information Age* (New York: Longman, 1982).

Hawken, P., Ogilvy, J., and Schwarts, P., *Seven Tomorrows* (New York: Bantam Books, 1982).

Nora, S., and Minc, A., *The Computerization of Society* (Cambridge, MA: MIT Press, 1980).

Toffler, A., *The Third Wave* (New York: William Morrow and Company, Inc., 1980).

Williams, F., *The Communications Revolution* (New York: Mentor Books, 1982).

CHAPTER TWO

COMPUTER GRAPHICS

This year's hot new car zooms out at you from the TV through cobalt blue grids in 3-D space.

Hundreds of numbers on an accountant's spreadsheet become a rainbow of floating pie charts on the boardroom's projection screen.

Dozens of video news shots are squeezed down to fit on one rotating model of the earth, promoting a network's hi-tech image.

An architect creates your new office building on a screen, then rotates it around so you can see what it will look like from the back, from the air, and from a worm's-eye view.

Each of these images is probably familiar to you, and you probably have an idea that computers play a role in them. In fact, computer graphics, from video games to business slides to special effects in feature films, may be one of the "friendliest" ways that computers have of communicating with us. But why employ a cold, number-crunching machine to do that which is supremely human: create art? The reasons vary, and we'll explore the myriad ways that computers can assist us in communicating using color, shape, and motion.

Computer-generated graphics have been around since the 1960s, but then, like everything related to computers, the process was expensive, technical, and time-consuming. With the increasing availability and interactivity of computers, however, a $14.5 billion market is predicted for all forms of computer graphics by 1990 (Knight, 1982), and soon they will be making a real dent in the traditional audio-visual markets of hand-drawn graphics, photographic slides, and even video shot with cameras.

CREATING COMPUTER GRAPHICS

How are computer images created? Well, the user inputs some kind of data into the system. This can come from a keyboard, by entering commands or numbers; from moving a cursor (a small square of light) on the screen using arrow keys on a keyboard, a joystick, or touching the screen itself; or using some kind of tablet that you trace upon. Computer graphics can be generated on small home computers using a general-purpose programming language (like BASIC) to draw colored lines, boxes, and so on. Or, you can purchase special software to load into a computer to allow you to draw on a screen using simpler, "bigger" commands than those available in general-purpose languages. Of course, to do some of the more sophisticated images, more expensive custom systems are used. They have special hardware to make the job of being artistic more natural and efficient, and they have powerful systems to create thousands of colors, manipulate and animate images, and produce very high-resolution pictures.

Once an image is created on a monitor and manipulated until it's satisfactory, it can be stored on a disk or tape. It can then be displayed to its audience on a video screen, using the computer to "play back" the image. Or, it can be recorded onto regular slide or motion-picture film or videotape using special devices. Printers or plotters can also be used to draw the image on a piece of paper or acetate.

You've undoubtedly seen some rather primitive computer graphics displayed in video games on small computers. The pictures are made of large squares, like mosaics, and the colors are rather limited. You've also seen beautifully colored and "smooth" computer animation in television commercials and films such as *Tron*. What's the difference?

Computer images are made up of *pixels* (for "picture elements"). Each pixel takes up computer memory; so do colors. Therefore, small home computers without much power can hold only a limited number of pixels and colors in memory, whereas expensive systems oriented specifically for creating images can hold many more pixels. The more pixels on the screen, the higher the *resolution,* or detail, of the image. A typical low-resolution image consists of about 250 pixels vertically by 250 pixels horizontally, for about 62,500 pixels to make up the entire picture. A medium-resolution image might be made up of about 250,000 pixels, but a high-resolution image like you see in computer-animated films and high-quality business slides may consist of as many as 16 *million* pixels!

Computer graphics systems have several means for displaying what they've created. Usually, an artist sits at a console and uses what looks like a TV screen to see what's being created. There are two kinds of screens that can be used:

raster monitors and *vector* monitors. A raster monitor is like a TV set, displaying pictures using combinations of hundreds of dots configured in lines that are scanned by an electron beam. To display a graphic, a raster monitor scans the entire screen, even if you've only drawn information in a small portion of it. A vector monitor, on the other hand, only knows how to draw lines—connecting point X to point Y. It only scans what you've created, so it's faster than the raster variety. The raster monitor is better for defining whole areas of color than the line-oriented vector screen. However, the raster monitor often makes diagonal lines look "jagged," like a stairstep (Bickford, 1983).

All of these technical processes, when used interactively, can offer the artist a new channel for creativity.

> "Remember, the computer just connects the dots." Those five little words are the simplest explanation of how the computer works. They also sum up the relationship between the artist and his new tool and should, once and for all, calm the nerves of graphics people who are afraid the computer is dehumanizing. . . . Like the abstract expressionist painters who thrived on drips and accidents to nourish their vision, computer artists have a ball doodling with options and improvising, like jazz musicians, at the controls . . . It is true, the computer is just another tool—but what a tool! (Muller, 1982)

WHY COMPUTER GRAPHICS?

Why use computer graphics when paintbrush and canvas have worked so well for so long? The first reason is quality. Today's graphics systems can produce 16 million different colors, with rich tones and subtle variations. Slides look especially crisp and clear when produced with one of these systems. Second, computer systems that create graphics are more efficient than traditional means. An artist can experiment on the screen without wasting sheets of poster board and bottles of paint; if you don't like an effect, you can just wipe it out! Titles can be automatically centered or lined up. Images can be duplicated, expanded, shrunk, rotated, colored differently, and so on. Libraries of symbols, corporate logos, or maps can be stored on disk and called up and positioned at will. Graphics production houses that turn out hundreds of slides and overhead transparencies have found that systems costing well over $100,000 have paid for themselves in increased productivity in no time at all. Computer animation systems require an artist only to create the initial and final positions of a figure; the computer "fills in" the rest of the movements to give a smooth, animated effect.

A third reason for using computer graphics is ease of editing and updating. In today's fast-paced world of business, figures are often out of date in a matter of days or hours. A computer-generated graphic can be stored on disk, and elements can be changed as quickly as you can process a simple title. Many companies store frequently used images, like a map showing branch locations. As new ones are added or old ones eliminated, updated graphics can be created in a matter of minutes with no waste of materials. This ease of editing also allows the artist to explore various effects without trying to conserve precious time and materials; different sizes, colors, and positions can be displayed rapidly until the most pleasing arrangement emerges. The last reason for using computer graphics is accuracy. To calculate percentages in a pie chart and then accurately represent them by hand is a tedious chore. To create a series of slides that, by dissolving from one to the other in a multi-image program create the effect of animation, is a complex process of lining up images perfectly—unless, of course, the computer does it for you. Computer artists can leave the mathematics and measuring to the computer, and use their time for designing more effective and artistic graphics.

Let's say you often make important business presentations using numeric data. Charts and graphs are effective means for getting your point across, and you feel that computer graphics might be a good way to have these produced. How would you go about it? You could simply take your ideas to a professional service bureau that creates computer graphics; here, an account executive can assess your needs and assign an artist to create slides, transparencies, or even images recorded on a computer disk to suit your situation. You might even interact with the artist while he or she tries different approaches to your graphic and co-produce the image! These graphics might range from $15 for a simple slide with a few words to $100 for complex charts or artistic sketches. If you need this service often enough, you might think of purchasing your own interactive, computer-graphic creation system. These range from $3,000 for a simple personal computer and graphics software package to over $100,000 for a sophisticated high-quality setup. Either of these systems will allow you to create images and display them on a screen. Only some are capable of transmitting that information to a film recorder or video tape recorder so that they can be displayed in another medium, such as slides, film, or video. Buying a high-quality film recorder to shoot your slides from a high-resolution display, for instance, is not an inexpensive proposition. If you want to turn your rather low-cost graphics created on a small system to slides, you can buy systems from companies like Genigraphics, Dicomed, and Visual Horizons that allow you to send your electronic data to them to be turned into slides or transparencies. This can be done by a phone hookup between your small computer and their film recorder, or you can physically provide them with the diskette on which the data for your graphics is saved. Only high-volume slide users or those with special security concerns usually purchase a complete setup including a film recorder.

Standard Oil Company of Indiana was one of the first large corporations to employ computer graphics. From 1972 to 1975, their use of business graphics rose from 441 to 25,300 slide projects. At this time, the company purchased a Genigraphics slide creation system. It allowed them to produce 19,656 slides per year, which was within 1,000 of 1974's total slide art output produced by 16 artists. A Genigraphics slide costs them approximately $15.60 to produce, compared with an average of $33.70 doing slides manually or $59.10 having slides produced by an outside studio. On that basis, they saved $181,000 over manual production and $435,000 over outside studio production in one year, even when producing only 10,000 slides per year. In a few years, they were producing over 20,000 slides per year and doubling their savings (Fortney, 1977).

CAN THE AVERAGE PERSON LEARN TO MAKE COMPUTER GRAPHICS?

In many beginning "computer literacy" classes, students are first exposed to creating computer graphics, because creating

FIGURE 2-1 Figures 2-1 and 2-2 show business graphics slides (courtesy of Genigraphics, Inc.).

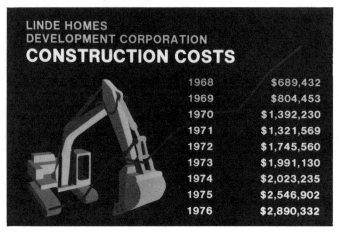

images may be least like the codified programming that many novices fear. An easy way to begin is with a simple software package for a personal computer. Most of these allow you to move the cursor, or "marking spot," around the screen and sketch by connecting points, not unlike the children's sketching toy of a few decades ago. By typing in a few commands, like R for rectangle, the computer will draw you a box using two diagonal points you've specified. Similarly, you can draw

FIGURE 2-2

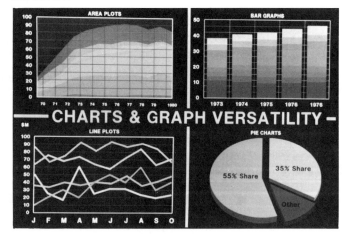

FIGURE 2-3 Media designer using Genigraphics system (courtesy of OmniCom Associates).

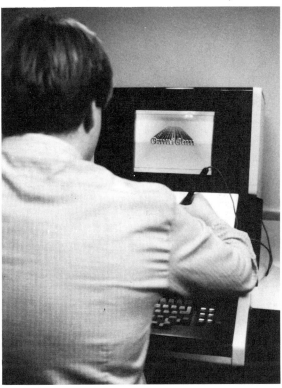

circles, triangles, lines, and polygons by merely plotting the corners and pressing a key. Depending upon your software and computer, various colors can be selected. Most packages also allow you to type in words and select from various type styles, or fonts. Most of these packages sell for about $50 and are probably cheaper in the long run than buying paper and crayons! The images can be stored on a diskette to be appreciated later by the creator's grandparents or business colleagues. Some programs allow you to create a computer "slide show" that automatically cycles through the images either at a specified interval or upon pressing a controller connected to the computer. In fact, many businesses are skipping the process of turning all computer images into slides and are presenting graphics directly on large, high-quality video screens.

FIGURE 2-4 Pages from a business graphics manual
(courtesy of Genigraphics, Inc.).

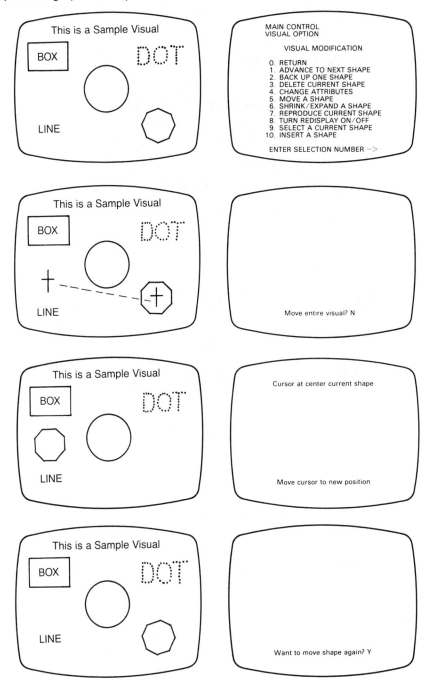

MOVING A SHAPE

Now let's move the polygon to another location in the visual. Select "5" from the modify menu. The steps are:

1. You don't want to move the entire visual at this point—only the polygon. The prompt already shows "N" for "NO", so just press the ENTER key.

2. Move the cursor near the center of the polygon. You may want to use the grid—ctrl & G here.

3. Move the cursor to a new location on the screen and press ENTER to move the polygon.

4. You have the option to move the shape again. Change the "N" to "Y" and move the polygon back to its original location.

Slightly more sophisticated packages allow you to create "business graphics," the standard charts and graphs used to display financial and scientific numerical information. Instead of drawing each bar in a bar chart by hand and calculating how high it should be, for example, business graphics programs create charts out of data you fill in. You input the numbers, let's say, of your volume of sales over the past four years, and the system automatically creates a line chart, bar chart, or pie chart. Some systems take in information from a business package like VisiCalc and generate graphics from your formulas. The resulting graphics can be displayed directly, printed onto paper to be included in a report, or in some packages, transferred to a film recorder to make slides or a video tape recorder to be included in a video program. These systems are easy to use for the administrative assistant or business person. They require no "programming" knowledge and enable the efficient creation of graphics that are easier to digest than rows of numbers. In fact, using these systems, you can take your computer into a meeting and input a variety of data on the spot. The computer can do the resulting calculations and formulas and display them in graphic form. These systems can speed decision-making and facilitate "what-if" exploration of ideas.

Not only is a knowledge of programming unnecessary to use these graphics systems, in many you don't even have to remember simple commands. Many like the Series 1000 System by Genigraphics, are menu-driven, that is, you just select from options presented to you on the screen. This system uses an IBM Personal Computer outfitted with extra memory, a hard disk for storing large amounts of data, and a special high-resolution color display.

Of course, a menu-based system like this one can offer you only a limited number of choices. More expensive and complex systems use specialized software and hardware. They take more training to use but offer more extensive and artistic capabilities. Images can be rotated, duplicated, and their colors changed among millions of shades by merely moving a stylus over a tablet. One striking effect often used in advertising presentations is a word with many "shadows" in different shades. This technique, called "space color," is easy to produce. You merely create the first word and pick out its color; you then duplicate the word, move it up and "behind" the first, shrink it down slightly, and change the color again. Then, using one command, the computer automatically fills in the rest of the copies of the word, gradually changing the size and shading of each copy.

GRAPHICS IN 3-D AND MOTION

The next stage of elaboration in computer graphics is 3-D modeling. By inputting formulas and parameters, designers can create objects with mass and depth and move those objects in space. This function is used in many of the animation scenes of electronically created films.

> In *Tron* . . . a computer programmer becomes trapped in the deadly world of a video arcade game. Actually, *Tron's* premise is not as fantastic as it seems. Many scenes did, in fact, occur inside a computer—not that of a video game, but of a powerful computer-aided design system [SynthaVision] . . . MAGI animators built *Tron's* props and scenery out of spheres, cones, cylinders, and other mathematically defined solid shapes stored in the system's memory. Then, acting on motion, lighting, and camera angle instructions, the system automatically animated and "filmed" scenes, recording the results on color film. (Kinnucan, 1982)

Once created, solid shapes can easily be animated by using the computer. To do traditional animation by hand, 24 drawings per second must be created, each showing objects moving just slightly to create the illusion of continuous motion. A 90-minute animated film can use over 130,000 hand-drawn frames! In commercial animation studios, the most experienced artists draw the "extremes," or key positions, for each character. Assistants called "in-betweeners" fill in the movements between each extreme, and even less skilled personnel ("opaquers") color in each cell. As early as the late 1960s, experiments were conducted to see how computers could help with the more routine chores. Today, most of the in-betweening for Hanna- Barbera Studios is done by computer systems developed in part by Cornell University's Computer Graphics Lab.

[In] computer assisted key-frame animation . . . the animator enters the lines ("strokes") in the picture in a certain order. When the next key frame is entered, the order in which the lines are traced can be used to determine the correspondence between the two extremes. The first stroke in the first key frame will be gradually transformed into the first stroke in the second key frame. The animator must make sure he draws exactly the same number of strokes in the destination frame as in the source frame; otherwise the computer would not be able to match [them]. (Booth, Kochanek, and Wein, 1982)

Computers can also help filmmakers do "tricks" such as those in the early *King Kong* film. To make the ape climb the Empire State Building, the filmmakers had to carefully shoot two films and make a "composite," or double exposure, in the lab. Today the computer can be used to insert or delete any given information from a film. This technique is used to "colorize" black-and-white films. You tell the system what color each object should be, and it can figure out where to put the colors, even as the objects move and turn within a frame. Pacific Electric Pictures has a system that allows you, for instance, to remove rooftop antennas from Dickensian street scenes. "After making these changes by hand on certain key frames, the computer program is 'smart' enough to follow through the patching operation on the other frames in the scene" (Sorensen, 1983).

Many of the special effects you see in video, as well as film, are the result of digital processing. For many years now, television stations and corporate video studios have used electronic typewriters, *character generators,* to put words on the screen. These are typically used in making ending credits, creating simple words-only graphics, and in identifying interviewees by the addition of a subtitle. Over the past decade, these simple character generators have become increasingly complex, allowing you to store previously written words on a cassette tape or a computer disk, expanding the range of type fonts and colors available, and adding often-used pictures, like rain clouds or football helmets, to their character sets. Personal computers can be used to generate simple TV graphics, but most do not output signals compatible to our broadcast standard (NTSC in the United States). You can add conversion units to some of these computers to make them "work" in a video studio setup, but many of these conversion packages cost as much as the basic computer itself (Allen, 1983).

In industrial/corporate video productions, the same systems used by stations can be just as useful. Computer graphics are replacing a lot of "talking heads" of many major corporations with concise visuals. The economy of use is also the same—most corporate producers "need it yesterday." An example of this is the Syntex logo, combined with a package of animated charts, graphs, and titling which had a 7-day turnaround. The producer presented his client with action graphics at a reasonable billing and everyone was happy. (Watkins, 1983)

In most commercial TV programs today, you see special effects like pictures being "squeezed" and moved around the frame. This is also done by computer manipulation. These digital effects devices, made by a few video companies like Ampex, MCI/Quantel, and Adda, store video images line by line in a digital form. Once stored this way, they can be manipulated (moved, expanded, rotated, shrunk, and so on). Since many of these systems cost over $100,000, they are used primarily by large TV stations and networks and by large production houses (Costello, 1982; Watkins, 1983).

Sophisticated image manipulation requires huge computer power. The Cray Research X-MP/22 machine is one of the most powerful computers in the world, with a price tag of over $12 million. One of the first models was bought by a Hollywood studio, Digital Productions, to create full-screen computer simulations. The Cray will allow the group to create images with a resolution of 24 million pixels per frame. "To create one frame, suppose the computer needs to make only 10 calculations to determine the value of each pixel. Commercial motion pictures run at 24 frames per second. Repeating the entire procedure for every frame, it would take $24 \times 10 \times 24{,}000{,}000$ or 5,760,000,000 calculations to produce one second's worth of film" (Schadewald, 1983).

Digital Productions (founded by two computer animation pioneers in their 30s, Gary Demos and John Whitney, Jr.) has produced a completely computer-synthesized film, and has visions of more personalized graphic adventures. "You just connect your personal computer to the Cray, tune in the cable channel, and become part of the movie," says Demos. "Instead of buying pay-TV movies, you pay Digital Productions for interactive movies that you're part of. We present generic possibilities, and you create variations based on your personality and abilities. You control things, create a custom movie that will never be seen by anyone else." Demos' partner, John Whitney, says, "Within this decade, the best in entertainment will be synonymous with high technology. . . . This will engender entirely new kinds of story writing and filmmaking; new words will enter the vocabulary of visual storytelling and computer imagery will increase in sophistication as the new producers and directors who are now entering the business learn to exploit these powerful tools of simulation." (Youngblood, 1983)

The Secret Synapse*

As an artist and computer animator, I feel obliged to warn you that there is nothing particularly easy about making computer animation, after all, things which are more complicated are usually less reliable.

*by Judson Rosebush.

FIGURE 2-5 Figures 2-5 through 2-10 show stills from animated commercials (courtesy of Judson Rosebush, Digital Effects, Inc.).

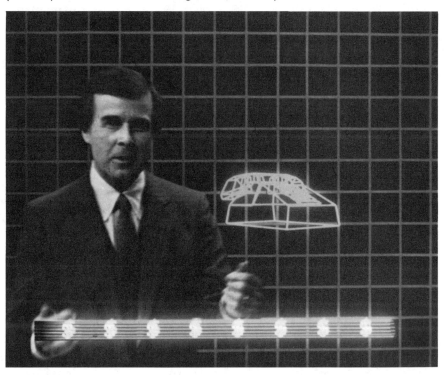

FIGURE 2-6

(a)

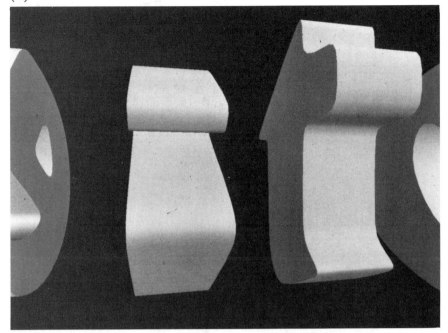

(b)

(c)

FIGURE 2-7

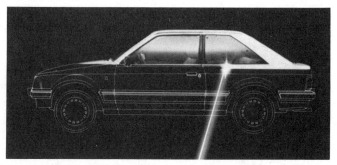

FIGURE 2-8

FIGURE 2-9

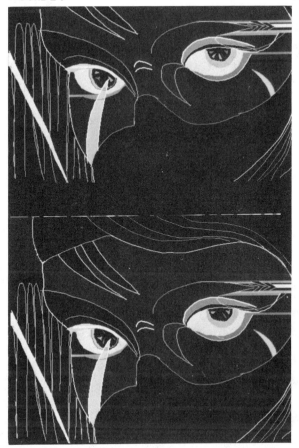

This is speaking off the record, of course, because officially my topic claims "you don't have to be a programmer to create computer art—but it helps."

There is something very special about computer graphics. First of all, especially for the graphic artist, it is a new medium. It is not film or video or blueprints; it is a whole new way of describing pictures and environments. Because it is intrinsically different, it does different things. For one thing, it is interactive. For another, it can be combined with modeling, simulation and analysis—the essential elements of CAD/CAM applications. Other differences are manifested in how pictures are created, transmitted and stored. As a medium, computer graphics is like clay—something you can add to and subtract from. It is, of course, also full color, and it can have a temporal variable.

FIGURE 2-10

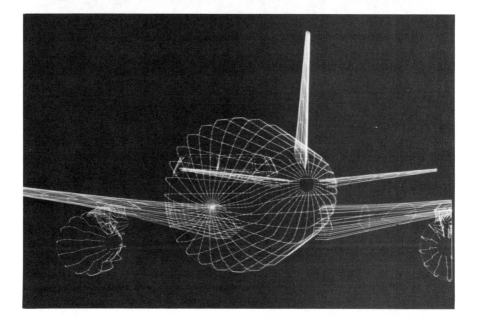

One of our first temptations with a new medium is to emulate old media: some of us have built computer-assisted cell cartoon systems. We have built graphic arts workstations that let us do make-up, illustration, and "painting." Yet even with paint systems, individual styles emerge and the machine surprises us with new techniques, which is fine. It is not enough for a machine to replicate a state of affairs—its introduction must synergize new expressions if it is to be seriously considered. Mark Lindquist's *Video-drome* is an example of this.

Three-dimensional graphics have attracted much of our fancy too—especially with our thrust, as a community, to dissect visual reality and express it as algorithms. I suspect questing reality is like Zeno's paradox: you may keep halving the distance to it but you never quite get there. Besides, reality already exists. Computer graphics can provide surreality, as well as a special twist through to the other side of your mind.

We begin doing this by writing computer graphics programs that model or replicate the way we perceive things visually. In the process of doing this, we resort to a notational system, a descriptive language, a mathematics which is expressed as computer programs.

In their first generation, these programs or expressions are merely descriptive logical models of the world. But in their second iteration this description undergoes a compaction or a crystallization along mathematical planes of thought instead of visual perception planes. Suddenly, we begin to manipulate this contraption mathematically and computationally, instead of visually. That is, instead of saying, "the surface of that object needs to be rougher," we say something like, "let's perturb some normals," whatever that means. Suddenly, we are off in a different world and for an instant we are conversing in that new world to effect a change that was visually conceptualized in the traditional real-world language.

The effect of this switch is an ability to manipulate a new world language which effects visual changes in the traditional world. But because the controls have a different bias, it is quite likely the results might appear accidental or unpredictable. The reason the result is a surprise is because the effect was not a candidate for visual manipulation, given our ways of dealing with the traditional visual world. It is our ability to manipulate the latent symbolic structure of an image that provides one reason why computers stimulate creativity.

In conclusion, I suggest you consider the possibility that computer graphics is not an emerging technology but already in its golden age. Our work, especially that which is image oriented, may soon be artifacts. I do not profess to know the future, but its media will probably involve a more flexible screen, spatial (volumetric) displays, and interaction that will probably involve feeling shapes. In the short term, all would seem to involve computer pictures.

How does somebody get into the interactive graphics business? Many people now in Hollywood or Madison Avenue got their

start with a contract from the Defense Department in the 1960s and 1970s. Dave Evans and Ivan Sutherland started a computer graphics program at the University of Utah to create a flight simulation system. As a result, they developed their own system and started their own company, and now Evans and Sutherland is a household word among the computer graphics and computer-assisted-design crowd. James Blinn came through their program at Utah, spent some time at the New York Institute of Technology, and went on to create computer simulations for the Jet Propulsion Lab in California. His creations of what Saturn must look like from a spacecraft flying by were so beautiful and lifelike that they made the covers of many major magazines. Another Utah protégée, Lance Williams, also went to the New York Institute of Technology to produce the first completely computer-generated animated film, *The Works* (Rivlin, 1983).

In addition to creating fanciful science-fiction films, 3-D modeling has more practical functions. The "hottest" of these is CAD/CAM (Computer-Aided Design/Computer-Aided Manufacturing). These systems allow automatic generation of engineering plans, architectural blueprints, and mechanical drawings. Once generated, these systems can control manufacturing systems to build what's been displayed.

To create 3-D images, you need to specify x, y, and z coordinates: the z-axis specifies the "depth" of the figure. By connecting coordinates, a three-dimensional object, or polyhedron, is created in outline. Polyhedra created this way look like a "wireframe" of an object.

> After the animator/programmer is assured that the wireframe object is constructed correctly . . . calculations called "alogrithms" can be applied. These include perspective and hidden line removal—the elimination of lines of the far side of the object, which our eyes would not normally see. Others involve making the object appear solid by filling in the polygons, adding color, and then calculating the effect of light, shading and shadows. . . . Some of the recent advances . . . include creating metallic textures, mapping two-dimensional images or patterns on three-dimensional objects and "smooth" or "continuous" shading. . . . (Bickford, 1983)

One 3-D modeling system has been designed with architects specifically in mind. The Arrigoni *Touch 'N Draw* system was created by a consulting engineer, David Arrigoni, who has a background in electronics, engineering, painting, and programming. He worked with a team of environmental engineers and architects to create a computer-assisted-design system for buildings in interiors. His system in its normal configuration sells for under $100,000. Arrigoni decided that this was the "magic number" because "it can be purchased on a five-year lease purchase plan and the amortization payments for each year are about equal to what a designer or draftsman would be paid. If the system can be made to do work equivalent to two or three workers, then the efficiencies are raised even higher." (Borrell, 1982)

According to the Arrigoni group, many small architectural firms are benefiting from its automation system. Bill Bergenthal runs a one-man architectural firm, A2D2, from his home in Anchorage, Alaska. He didn't want to have to hire temporary help during the busy season, so instead he bought a Touch 'N Draw system. ". . . the system is configured to be an electronic extension of normal drafting tools: the digitizer is the drafting table; the cursor is the drawing implement; the disk is a sheet of paper; the plotter produces final copy; and the Touch Control Station and Touch 'N Draw software perform the details of drafting, leaving the architect or engineer free to create." Bergenthal likes the flexibility the system gives him. "It's easy for me to change a drawing if I don't like the way something is working out—I don't spend hours erasing it! And I don't have to live with a design solution that might not be perfect. I can modify at will to come up with the best solution in a fraction of the time I would have spent using manual drafting methods" (Arrigoni, 1983).

Computers may not make all of us Michelangelos, but they certainly offer assistance to those of us with some artistic abilities and let the rest of us, at least, make clean and accurate bar charts. Like many other aspects of computers, electronic graphics systems may allow us to work more creatively and efficiently. They may even enhance interaction between artists instead of, as many people fear, isolating individuals. For instance, a network of computer graphics firms in Ohio, Texas, and Washington, D.C. are sharing resources and equipment by going on-line with each other. They can ship each other artwork over telephone lines, allowing them to see techniques

created by individual artists. When one branch is especially busy, "roughs" can be sent by express mail, courier, or by telecopier, and finished products can be executed by another colleague. The data for the finished art can be shipped back to the originator's studio and shot on their film recorder (Rasmussen, 1982). If a client, for instance, is making a hurried business presentation across the country, he or she can hand a rough sketch to a computer graphics house at home base. The production house can then create the graphic and send the data to a branch where the presentation will be made. They can print the slide or vu-graph, and the client can pick it up at his or her destination.

Graphics are not only important in and of themselves but are integral parts of other computer-based technologies, such as computer-assisted instruction, videotex, and simulation. As we'll see, attractive graphics can enhance communication and, with today's new systems, can be as easily created as typing a few words or tracing an outline on a sketch pad.

REFERENCES

Allen, D., "Low-Cost Computer Graphics," *Videography* (October, 1983), pp. 40–44.

Arrigoni Computer Graphics, Inc., "Alaska Architect Credits CADD for Handling Increased Business Without Increased Hiring," unpublished paper, 1983.

Bickford, S., "Coming of Age," *Audio-Visual Communications* (April, 1983), pp. 16–19.

Booth, K., Kochanek, D., and Wein, M., "Computers Animate Films and Video," *IEEE spectrum* (February, 1982), pp. 44–51.

Borrell, J., "From User to Manufacturer," *Computer Graphics World* (April, 1982), pp. 47–52.

Costello, M., "The Digital Video Effects Universe," *Videography* (November, 1982), pp. 35–41.

Fortney, J., "How to Use Computer Graphics for Cost Savings: A Narrative Case Study in Short Story Form," unpublished paper, Standard Oil Company of Indiana, 1977.

Kinnucan, P., "Solid Modelers Make the Scene," *HighTechnology* (July/August, 1982), pp. 38–44.

Knight, K., "Coming Attractions," *Audio-Visual Communications* (December, 1982), pp. 26–30.

Muller, M., "Connecting Dots, or Graphics by Computer," *Upper and Lower Case: The International Journal of Typographics* (September, 1982), p. 36.

Rasmussen, R., "Design Network Thrives: Computer Graphics and Telecommunications Are The Key," *Computer Graphics News* (January/February, 1982), p. 3.

Rivlin, R., "Filming by Computer," *Technology Illustrated* (February, 1983), pp. 26–30.

Schadewald, R., "Crays in Tinseltown: Why Image Synthesis Takes So Much Computer Time," *Technology Illustrated* (February, 1983), p. 32.

Sorensen, P., "Far from the Matting Crowd: The Digital Film Compositor," *Technology Illustrated* (February, 1983), pp. 34–35.

Youngblood, G., "Next . . . Total Scene Simulation," *Video Systems* (February, 1983), pp. 18–27.

Watkins, R., "Characters in the News," *Video Systems* (October, 1983), pp. 46–50.

CHAPTER THREE

VIDEOTEX

It's a typical weekday morning. After downing a leisurely cup of coffee, you stroll over to your personal computer. Wonder who's sent mail overnight? Let's sign on to your information utility and check your E-Mail. Sally, your colleague on the other coast, suggests that you book a flight and join her in Washington for a business meeting. Afterwards, she says, there are probably some great new restaurants to try out or perhaps a concert at the Kennedy Center. And remember, she says, to bring your information on the latest manufacturing technologies in the semiconductor industry.

OK. First, let's look over what today's weather will be. Your modem automatically dials up the local weather bureau. Oh, no, the map looks like you're in for another hot one! Well, Washington sounds like fun, but you'll need to make flight reservations in a hurry; a holiday weekend is coming up. Pressing a few more keys on your computer, you can peruse the airline schedules. Don't forget your credit card number; punching it in will reserve your seat on a Super-Saver. Restaurants . . . let's call up the *Washington Post* restaurant review from last Sunday, and while we're at it, let's check into the theater offerings in Washington.

It's getting hot already! You really should look into getting another air conditioner. Sign on to the shopping channel on your cable TV; maybe there are some units on sale this week. Yep, looks like there are, but they're at the store all the way across town. No worry—just press a button, and they'll deliver it and charge your account automatically. Before the morning's over, though, better check out your database and pull in some information on those semiconductors!

If all of this sounds like science fiction, it *can* be done and *is* being done in living rooms all over the world. Teletext/ videotex systems provide printed and graphic information on a TV screen, either through wires, cable, or through broadcast. There are a number of kinds of systems terms and techniques involved, but they have a lot in common. Tyler (1979) defined the technology as "systems for the widespread dissemination of textual and graphic information by wholly electronic means, for display on low-cost terminals (often suitably equipped television receivers), under the selective control of the recipient, and using control procedures easily understood by untrained users."

Rather than a wholly new technology, teletext/videotex could be likened to a merger of the coded words of telegraph with the instantaneous two-way selective contact of the telephone and the wide coverage and color pictures of broadcast television.

TERMINOLOGY

As do most of the interactive technologies, this one goes by many different names: videotex, videotext, teletext, viewdata, on-line information service, and so on. As the terminology becomes somewhat standardized, *teletext* (like *tele*vision) is one-way selectable print/graphic information, whereas *videotex* indicates a two-way information system. It may also be used to encompass the broad category of all consumer-oriented information services.

These systems appear on the screen in two basic forms. Sending strings of white-on-black characters scrolling onto the screen are the *on-line information services*. This format was developed from teletype and is oriented to displaying textual information. Of course, on the other end is a large, powerful computer with a number of simultaneous users, rather than another person at the teletypewriter. These systems use the phone lines and a "modem," originally developed to enable the deaf to use phone lines for teletype communication, and a standard teletype code for letters (ASCII). These services can be accessed by nearly any terminal or computer/modem without hardware modification. The second variety is oriented to the color graphics and screen format of the TV set and will be referred to in this chapter as *videotex*. This color-graphic system can be selectable, one-way or two-way (interactive). Not surprisingly, decoding graphics and color is more complicated and, of course, system developers all had their pet solutions to these problems. As a result, computers differ radically in the ways the reproduce color and graphics. In addition, there are several ways of encoding and transmitting these screens, so they require either a special terminal, or adapter hardware or software for a microcomputer to fit the particular standard used.

Tydeman, et al. (1982) list the following as characteristics of this rather broad technology:

- It is essentially a *medium-free* electronic technology encompassing various forms of information transmission, including scrolling or recorded voice, captioning, teletext, narrowband videotex, wideband videotex, and personal computers with fully on-line database systems. The transmission is by one or more electronic means, such as radio wave, TV signal, coaxial cable, copper wire, optical fiber, microwave, or satellite.
- There is an orientation toward widespread dissemination of textual and graphic information.
- The information is under user control.
- The technology represents an array of services, such as information retrieval, transactions, messaging, computing, and telemonitoring.
- The system is relatively low in cost for the user.
- Rather than being a new technology, it is the product of merging communication and computing systems.

Although developing in the United States, these systems have already been put into place more extensively in Canada and Europe, where the government usually coordinates mail, phone, and telegraph services, as in Great Britain. Telecom (the postal and telephone service) has established Prestel, a videotex service. The beginnings of videotex occurred in 1974, when a British engineer, Sam Fedida, demonstrated a working model. By 1976, public testing of the system was underway, and by 1979, the system known as Prestel was commercially available. At the same time, British teletext, known as Ceefax and Oracle, was being developed by the two broadcasting entities BBC and IBA. The Department of Communications in Canada also developed an integrated videotex service using a standard called Telidon in the late 1970s, and the early 1980s saw similar ventures in most of the major European countries and Japan.

Like many developing interactive technologies, videotex seems to be a medium in search of its identity. To be able to instantly send "electronic mail," pay bills, download computer programs, read current newspaper and magazine articles, order airline tickets, and keep up-to-the-minute tabs on the stock market are attractive and currently available options on many systems. There are, of course, poorly designed and trivial services. The pros and cons of public versus commercial development are being replayed in the case of videotex as well: Should it be a public service and funded as a nonprofit government agency or developed as a commercial commodity in an entrepreneurial style?

This is exactly the situation with which developers, information providers, equipment manufacturers, and information transmission utilities are struggling. What will make videotex attractive (i.e., profitable)? A number of different answers emerge. Low-cost receiving hardware is certainly desirable if the medium is to achieve a significant market. This means either very inexpensive decoders/terminals dedicated to videotex, or adapters for microcomputers, which many people already own. All can be displayed on a home TV. But the decoder and/or consumer-information sending device varies from system to system. In broadcast teletext, the decoder is a simple, inexpensive key pad that attaches through an adapter into a regular TV. It receives, or "grabs," screens or frames as they are sent and gives the user a choice among available screens. However, teletext is *not* two-way. The user can merely select screens and not send information back to the source or to other users. Some videotex systems use a specially designed decoder/keyboard by which information can be received and sent. Since these systems use phone lines, they are two-way, and users can order services, select among a large number of databases or screens, and communicate on-line with the "host" computer or other users. The custom decoders are usually easy to use, small, and relatively inexpensive. Other videotex systems use "dumb terminals," which are like computer keyboards and screens without the computer "brains." Of course, a regular personal computer can also be used with these systems. While they can be more expensive than the special decoders, they are also multipurpose and already exist for other uses in many homes and offices.

But where does videotex fit into the information environment? Is there a need to clutter the average home and office with yet another electronic gadget?

Since its commercial introduction in 1976, videotext has become a metaphor for a new world of information dissemination: a world in which text and pictures are stored as electronic impulses, transmitted in seconds at the touch of a button, displayed in color in millions of homes and offices. In this metaphor, videotext stands for the future, whereas older methods of transmitting information—mainly print on paper—represent the past. Those who develop videotext systems, or who advocate their use, do so with the unspoken conviction that the technology is an improvement over printed communications. (Sigel, 1983)

There are certainly a number of advantages of such electronic information over traditional print or broadcast media. First, information can be updated and accessed instantly, without taking time to set type, print articles or books, and distribute these physical packages of words. Second, electronic information can be personalized. A system can be tailored to your interests and needs and automatically display, record, or print out just that information. Third, it eliminates the simple clutter of print. Thousands of articles can be accessed instantly with a small terminal, and only select information can be chosen to print. Fourth, unlike the other "instant" media of radio and TV, videotex is relatively inexpensive for the information provider. Very few of us can afford to buy a broadcast station, but anyone with a home computer, a telephone line, a modem allowing the computer to "talk" on the phone line, and some good thoughts can become an *information provider,* or *IP,* either by starting a service or creating a section

FIGURE 3-1 Figures 3-1 and 3-2 show videotex screens created for AT&T (courtesy of Maria Manhattan).

FIGURE 3-2

of an existing service. Even frame-creation stations for the design and execution of elaborate graphics are not prohibitively expensive.

Electronic Artistry*

During the last two years I have been fortunate to work on one of the great experiments of our time. That experiment is the exploration of a field that promises to put us all on-line to each other and to large databases filled with vast amounts of information. That field is called Videotex—two-way communication using phone lines and satellites.

Videotex will service us in many ways. It can find an Italian restaurant within 3 blocks of your home (not to mention providing a review of the restaurant, a peek at the menu, and the ability to make reservations); or perhaps you would like to thumb through the Electronic Cookbook in search of a special holiday recipe.

Videotex is still in its infancy and is dealing with both technological and conceptual problems that will ultimately determine its success or failure. It needs a chance to develop in every way. Presently it is an imitative medium trying to be a bit of many things that are already familiar to us: newspapers, magazines, banks, etc. Eventually, we will

*by Maria Manhattan

find out what it does best. It will develop its unique point of view, style, and sense of drama. Minds will be opened and new ideas will be tried. Artists from all media must be let loose with the idea and the equipment. People today are audio/visually sophisticated: for Videotex to hold a person's attention, the information presented must be pleasant to watch, entertaining, and most of all, compelling. We've got to *want* to watch it!

Videotex was conceived of as an information medium. Information, however, does not necessarily equal boring! And information can be transmitted in any number of ways besides the obvious use of screens filled with text.

Because of the eyestrain involved with reading reflected light flickering at the rate of 30 frames per second, no one is going to want to read anything too weighty off the tube. Graphics, in fact, read so much better than text—they are legible and enjoyable to watch. Let's take a lesson from political cartoonists who say so much through their graphics with a minimum of words.

The most exciting part of being involved in this industry is working in computer graphics. Some of the machines that create the graphics are truly remarkable—magical almost. I was hooked from the first time I was able to create my Nancy Reagan caricature and then within seconds change the color of her dress and hair, even take her hair off and move it across the screen. By the time I sized and inverted the image (leaving Nancy standing on her head for a yoga lesson), there was no turning back.

The bigger machines that are used to interface with film and video are even more amazing. Some can automatically shade a picture if you simply tell it the direction of your light source. And of course that shading can be airbrushed, or hardedged. Some machines can produce a very painterly, brushlike effect. I find the idea of drawing with light very fascinating. Actually, we're drawing by telling the computer to deposit light at specified points for particular amounts of time—what a concept!

Computer graphics provides a wonderful new medium for artists to explore. We must now create works of art for this medium and expand the vision of what can be done with it.

It will be a little while before Videotex is desired with the kind of enthusiasm people shared when they bought their first telephones and TV sets. But I do think that in the future, we will accept it in some form as an ordinary part of our lives.

Picture a network of computers that allows ordinary people to do extraordinary things . . . like reach out and access information gathered thousands of miles away. Send messages around the globe, with imaginative graphics in brilliant color. Browse through a catalog, order merchandise, and pay the bill with a few quick keystrokes. Comparison shop for groceries from home. Study the latest development in cancer research. Or offer hard-won knowledge to the rest of the world.

This remarkable network is part of a trend that will revolutionize our society. At this moment in history, the cost of computer and communications equipment is falling, as their power grows astronomically. This trend continually delivers computing power to people who could not afford it before. Ultimately, it will democratize the power of the computer . . . and greatly increase every user's ability to achieve important personal goals.

This statement is not from a study of the future, a political campaign, or a science fiction novel. It is from an advertising brochure developed by the Digital Equipment corporation (DEC) and widely distributed at the Videotex '83 Conference in New York City. This language is indicative of promoters' and users' views of videotex. Most such brochures feature columns of technical specifications, descriptions of operating ease, and so on. Perhaps this medium, more than all others, is characterized not so much by hardware and programming as by its potential sociological and political implications. Alvin Toffler, in his best seller, *The Third Wave* explains how communications, made instant, efficient, and cheap by such technologies as videotex, will mark the third wave of civilization. It will "wash over" the entire culture, with changes as sweeping as those which the previous waves of agriculturalism and industrialism brought about. He speculates about the revolutions of "electronic cottage" work, schooling at home, and an electronic plebiscite running the government.

Although videotex visionaries are enthusiastic about the potentials of the electronic networks, the fact remains that the medium has not caught on in the decade or so of its existence. Many trials and experiments have been undertaken at great expense by such giants as Time/Life, CBS, and *Reader's Digest*. Certainly, some systems are squeezing out a profit. Others are heavily subsidized by government, yet others are seen as large R & D efforts in the hopes of striking it rich when the boom comes. Most commercial systems continue to operate because the essential equipment or information is already a part of another division of the company. For instance, Compu-Serve is owned by H & R Block, and this principally nighttime information service uses powerful computers being leased on a time-share basis to other companies during the day. The Time Teletext service, of course, has access to the news and information of the Time/Life publishing giant, which owns American Television and Communications (ATC), one of the country's largest cable television system owners, as well as Home Box Office (HBO), the world's largest pay-television program supplier. "ATC owns 119 cable systems in 33 states, and HBO has approximately 12 million subscribers. Time Incorporated is also the country's largest publisher of magazines and books and has a big stake in the impact of new media, so it is natural that electronic publishing would be of particular interest to the company" (Pfister, 1983). "*Reader's Digest* derives more than $1 billion in revenue from selling printed magazines and books to consumers around the world. If there is any likelihood that print will some day yield to electronics, isn't it prudent for the *Digest* to hedge its bets? For that huge publisher, spending a couple of million dollars on a venture like The Source is comparable to a homeowner's outlay of $500 annually for fire and theft insurance" (Sigel, 1983).

There are certainly several reasons why the medium hasn't reached the level of some predictions. Probably most importantly, we haven't quite figured out what to do with the medium. Just as the first films were stage plays recorded on celluloid, and the first TV programs were movies or radio with pictures, some videotex looks like a newspaper on a TV screen. Not many people will find that attractive for too long because it is quite laborious to read much text from a screen, and you certainly can't easily carry a terminal and monitor with you to read on the bus. Although the medium was originally designed primarily as a consumer-oriented service, most consumers don't have a need for such a quantity of tailored, instant information. Not only does even the prettiest teletext frame suffer from comparison with the full-color, sound, motion TV program, but the equipment needed to receive it is still a mystery to the average consumer. Most users are businesses who have a real need for instant updates on such information as hog futures and airline schedules, or those in the information industries who need to rapidly search out disparate information without the time and money involved in traveling even to the local public library. The next largest group of users is computer hobbyists for whom videotex is yet another thing one can do with the personal computer at a modest cost. On-line services allow users to "chat," meet new people, and share stories, much like citizen's band radio. Special-interest groups combine club meetings, newsletters, bulletin boards, conferences, and conversations electronically. On-line services also allow access to a large variety of programs and, in some cases, to the computing power and storage of a larger machine for those who have run out of software or computer memory. Other more advanced videotex features, such as the "shopping at home" transactions, electronic banking, and downloading whole software programs like video games, are still only in the experimental stages. Although they might make the medium more attractive than its print and broadcast competition, the fact remains that consumers don't "know" that they "need" these features yet.

Some people see videotex developing like a suburban shopping mall. The counterparts to the big department store will be the bank and mail order merchandiser. The equivalent to the many small shops surrounding the big store will be the various other videotex services. A user might not be willing to pay for just one of these, any more than he would be willing to travel to the shopping center to visit just one small store, but the totality of the services would snare him—or so the theory goes. (*High Technology,* 1983)

HOW VIDEOTEX IS CREATED

..---. . . .. ---.- was probably the first kind of videotex—words coded and sent along a wire as telegraph messages. The dots and dashes were, of course, made by sending patterns of electric current through a pair of wires using an off/on switch known as the telegraph key. Messages being received were heard as the clicks made by a small electromagnet at the other end of the wires. The system was made two-way by attaching either the key or the electromagnet to the wires for sending or receiving. All of the coding and decoding of words was through the skill of the telegrapher. Then too, early telegraphy was an on-line or real-time craft—you had to be there to get or send a message. A great boon to the telegraphers was a device that not only clicked, but also punched holes in a paper tape. This storage device reduced decoding errors and made receiving messages much more convenient. This same paper-punch system was adapted to send messages, too.

As simple as this early text-sending system seems to us today, it contains all the elements of the most futuristic teletext systems: message design, coding, transmission, decoding, and message storage on one or both ends. (Of course, the system goes back again in two-way systems, sharing the transmission medium or using an alternative one.) All interactive tele-communication technologies differ only in the particular ways they perform one or two of these functions.

We'll assume that the messages to be communicated on the system have been well designed to be attractive, interesting, and useful. (This is really the greatest challenge!)

Encoding usually begins by typing text screens into a terminal or microcomputer for ASCII services; this, plus a little "typewriter art," is all that needs to be done. If the screens are part of an interactive system, there are some branching instructions and information about dealing with user inputs. Color and graphics destined for a videotex system require some software and perhaps an electronic tablet to aid in their creation. These can be added to a microcomputer or be integral parts of a frame-creation terminal much like an interactive computer graphics system. The software assists in drawing shapes, moving them around the screen, changing their size, shape, and color, and so on. The tablet serves as a base for freehand drawing or tracing with a penlike control. This finished screen has been encoded as a series of numbers that will reconstruct the colored image on any compatible terminal. The encoded screens are delivered to the host system as a diskette or over phone lines from the IP's computer. The host system files the screens and sends them on request by the user.

Currently, videotex hitches a ride on the available trans-mission routes: TV-cable, the "airwaves," and telephone lines. In each case the string of numbers must be further coded into the kind of electronic information each route is "used" to carrying—like beeps on the phone lines or high frequency waves similar to those carrying sound and pictures. The encoder is associated with the host system. One-way or teletext services share space on the same channel as cable or broadcast programs by "inserting" these coded screens in the space between video frames you've seen as a black bar when a TV picture rolls. (This is how the system of closed-captioning for the hearing-impaired is transmitted.) Two-way or videotex systems use phone lines or require their own television channel— usually a cable one. The tradeoffs are that the teletext can piggyback a more or less free ride to anyone in broadcast range, but it is slower, one-way, and offers a limited choice of screens. Videotex, including ASCII text services over phone lines, is interactive, practically unlimited in database size, private, and potentially worldwide, but slow, especially for color graphics. Most services use one of the computer-oriented long-distance networks like Telenet or Tymnet so there are no separate toll charges. Finally, teletext using an entire cable channel is very fast and provides interaction, but only to those with a cable connection linked to that service.

For the ASCII services, decoding is accomplished by the modem, plus a few commands generated by the host system to fit the display onto your particular size screen or printer. Although ASCII is not an international standard, it is widely used in this hemisphere for computer-based telecommunication.

Videotext/teletext involves a more complex decoding situation. First, there are both graphics and color to be dealt with, creating a much more complex image out of those strings of numbers. Second, there are different coding/decoding systems or standards used in and advocated by different countries and companies. A North American Standard, however, appears to be emerging, but there are several in Europe. Third, there is still discussion about terminals versus microcomputers as receivers. Some favor special-purpose monitors and keyboards for teletext, but they are relatively expensive for dedicated hardware. Others point out that many already own computers that only need converters and that can store and create screens as well. Neither terminals nor converters are widely available at this time. All of these issues will mature and/or "shake out" as videotex/teletext applications come of age.

VIDEOTEX AND TELETEXT SERVICES : UNITED STATES

As of the beginning of 1984, the only commercially available videotex/teletext services in the United States were on-line information services that are ASCII (text-only) based. However, those ASCII services had a total of over 200,000 users and were growing quite rapidly.

These services include:

American Farm Bureau "Green Thumb" Service, operating in eight midwest states. Its services are free and it has about 400 users.

CompuServe (CompuServe Information Service), a comprehensive information service operated out of Columbus, Ohio. Their service includes abstracts of magazines and newspapers, bulletin boards, electronic mail, special-interest group sections, stock market prices, some games and educational programs, material from the *World Book Encyclopedia,* some home shopping, and a "CB," or group-chat option. CompuServe is accessed over regular phone lines, has over 50,000 users, and can use any personal computer or dumb terminal. The rates are $22.50/hour and $5/hour, depending upon the baud rate (speed of the incoming information) during evenings and weekends, and for a substantially higher price during regular business hours. CompuServe was reported to have 37,000 subscribers in the spring of 1983. (Hecht, 1983)

Dow Jones News/Retrieval service has been operating since 1977, although originally it was intended for brokers and professional investors only. Since 1980, it has actively sought out the "casual" investor, making its service easily accessible by phone through the popular personal computers. It has the largest number of subscribers of the U.S. databases (80,000 as of summer 1983), and covers not only financial news, but also articles in the *Wall Street Journal* and *Barron's,* movie reviews, sports reports, and on-line shopping.

The Source calls itself "America's information utility." Owned by *Reader's Digest,* it contains perhaps the broadest selection of databases of the U.S. videotex services. It can be accessed by any personal computer or dumb terminal and costs between $18 per hour and $4 per hour depending upon the time and the baud rate. Similar to CompuServe, Source offers electronic mail, bulletin boards, games, educational programs, news and financial information, downloading of programs, airline schedules, restaurant reviews, and job information. Source was reported to be losing money, but it had 25,000 subscribers as of spring 1983 (Hecht, 1983).

Professional Farmers of America (PFA) and PFA Instant Update are specialized services providing farmers with relevant information. The service uses TRS-80 computers exclusively and has about 2,500 users.

A number of teletext and videotex tests are being conducted throughout the United States. Bank projects include Citibank's "Homebase" in New York City, First Bank Systems' "First-hand" in North Dakota and Minnesota, First Interstate Bank's "Day and Night Video Banking" in California, Chemical Bank's "Pronto," and Chase Home Banking, both in New York City. Newspaper- and magazine-sponsored systems include "Homserv/Cox Index, Knight-Ridder's "Viewtron" in Florida, the *Advertiser—Tribune's* "A-T Videotext" in Tiffen, Ohio, and the *Times Mirror*/Infomart in California. Telecommunications companies such as AT&T/CBS and continental Telephone have also conducted trials. Time/Life conducted a large-scale trial of its cable-based teletext system. Unlike most other teletext systems, which use the vertical interval of a regular TV Channel to store a limited number of frames, the Time system used an entire cable channel. This enables the system to cycle four to five thousand frames instead of the one or two hundred available using only the few lines available in the vertical blanking interval.

Commercial broadcast stations, public television affiliates, and cable channels have also been involved in trying to exploit the teletext market. WFLD in Chicago introduced teletext magazines called *Keyfax* and *Night Owl*. As the station was picked up and rebroadcast by a number of cable operators, it was distributed on a national scale. Three Los Angeles stations, KNXT, KCET, and KNBC, began field tests of the French Antiope teletext system in 1981, and early the next year, the San Francisco station KPIX introduced a similar trial. A large publicly funded experiment through WETA, the public broadcast station in Washington, D.C., began in 1981 using the Canadian Telidon system. Southern Satellite Systems broadcasts Reuters' news wire over the vertical blanking interval of WTBS, the Turner Broadcasting "super station" picked up by a large number of cable stations. Rather than having homes equipped with decoders, the cable operators decode the signal and broadcast it over an empty channel. Pages change automatically—the home viewer has no control of what is displayed.

VIDEOTEX AND TELETEXT SERVICES : WORLDWIDE

European countries have led the field in establishing viable videotex and teletext services. In most cases, these systems are supported by the government (either the communications department or the PTT—Postal, Telephone, and Telegraph—commission). As discussed earlier, the pioneer British system, Prestel, has been the model for videotex throughout the world. Today it has over 25,000 users and supports not only publicly accessed databases, but CLGs, or closed user groups. These private groups allow limited access to information and conferencing and are used for such applications as training by Barlays Bank (Aldrich, 1982). The teletext services offered by the BBC and IBA have over one million users.

France has invested significant amounts of time and money to study videotex. In the early 1970s, the country established the French Center for the study of Telecommunications and Television (CCETT). Simon Nora and Alain Minc's (1980) plan to use both phone- and broadcast-based service on the Antiope standard is one of the most important documents in this new field. The Telesystems Eurodial system has over 5,000 users, and in 1982 the phone company started a project to equip phone users with electronic directories rather than printed phone books. These "Minitel" terminals cost less than $10 per month for business customers and are free for home users (Link, 1983). The goal is to equip all 30 million French telephone installations to electronic number retrieval by 1992.

Canada's efforts have been supported by their Department of communications as well as Bell Canada. Their system, Telidon, has more sophisticated graphics capabilities than Prestel and has become the basis for the U.S. North American Presentation Level Protocol (NAPLPS) standard. Infomart is the private software company involved in the various information delivery systems. Together with the Manitoba Telephone

Company, they have developed "Project Grassroots," aimed at rural farmers. It is distributed by both phone and cable and has over one thousand users. Infomart also has joint projects with the Canadian government to provide a free Canada Information Bank in public spots and also a free Teleguide to Ontario for tourists. Another system aimed at high-end businesses is Teleglobe "Novatex," providing up-to-the-minute financial news and enabling businesses to create impressive computer-based slide shows for meetings and presentations.

The Tele-Health Project:
Interactive Media for Public Health Education*
The Case of James T.

James T., an otherwise healthy man, has for three weeks now been feeling sad and guilty. He has trouble sleeping, very little appetite, and has interrupted his daily routine. Mr. T. is a 68-year-old male widower and lives with his married son, Paul. Although all the signs point to a possible depressive state, Paul is just beginning to suspect something is wrong because these manifestations did not appear all at once, and also because Mr. T. strongly denies any unusual feelings. Furthermore, he does not take well to being told to "pull himself together." This working-class family is not very familiar with psychological or medical culture. They need to know what to make of this situation and how to handle dad in order to help him.

What are Paul's options?

Options	Probable Outcome
1. Ask friends.	They have contradicting "opinions."
2. Call family doctor.	Suggests he sees a psychiatrist.
3. Call hospital.	Line is always busy.
4. Call private psychiatrist.	Thirty-day waiting period and $100 per 45-minute session.
5. Consult home videotex Tele-Health databank.	Immediate access to information tailored to Paul's specific needs.

For the purposes of the present introduction, Paul chooses to consult his videotex databank. This choice is also motivated by the fact that

*by Robert Perreault, M.D., F.C.R.P., and Michel Bourque, Ph.D.

Tele-Health is available for health education and information at the very time and place of highest user motivation. Inability to provide such focalized service constitutes one of the main drawbacks of traditional methods of health education. Furthermore, this computer-assisted approach offers as many individually tailored messages as there are users, as opposed to traditional mass media that provide a single message to a mass audience. This type of flexibility and adaptability seems particularly well suited to health crises, since such problems as Paul and his father are faced with usually seem to require attention at the most awkward moments such as late on Saturday nights.

Here is an excerpt from the interaction that follows Paul's consultation with the Tele-Health bank:

Tele-Health: Which of our programs would you like to consult today?

Paul: Depression

T.H.: People associate depression with sadness, solitude, fatigue and generally, "the blues." Personally, have you ever felt depressed?

Paul: I don't know.

T.H.: It is sometimes difficult to recognize the symptoms of depression. Still, it is very frequent: each year, in North America, a million and a half individuals are being treated for this illness. . .According to you, why do some individuals become depressed? Is it mostly because of their character or because they are living difficult situations?

Paul: Because of their character.

T.H.: You are partially right. Some people are more vulnerable to depression because of a biochemical unbalance. However, very often, depression is also a "reaction" to some external event occurring within a difficult situation. Would you like some examples?

Paul: No.

T.H.: Let me only point out that the same situation can be more depressing for a given individual than for another. The elderly are an illustration of this phenomenon. Would you care for more details?

Paul: Yes.

T.H.: The elderly often live through difficult situations:
onset of a serious or chronic illness
retirement
death of spouse

move into a nursing home

poverty, etc.

Moreover, the elderly are more fragile physically, making it more difficult to adjust to new situations. Also, they are destined to take more drugs, some of which cause depressive states. Would you like to see the list of these drugs?

Like a great many of today's futuristic scenarios, this one is presently being implemented. In a 24-month trial of home interactive television set-up by the Bell Canada Corp. in 500 Canadian homes, the health education material contributed by the authors' research group has consistently received the highest ratings. Also, a waiting-room application of the system has been implemented for hypertensive patients at the Clinical Research Institute of Montréal over the last three years. Through the system, patients have access to computers in the waiting room programmed to provide answers to health-related issues while the patients wait for their appointments. At this time, this high-penetration approach to consumer access to information is best made possible by the advent of videotex technology.

Videotex and Health Promotion

Also referred to as interactive television, videotex blends the well-documented appeal of television with the memory, intelligence and networking abilities of the computer. In the health field, the network of terminals linked to a central databank seems particularly well adapted to the network structure of most health care organizations. Furthermore, the imperatives of scientific validation and rapid turnover of information warrant the use of centralized databanks for the greater majority of health education needs. Whereas mass media are good at offering a single message to a great number of people, interactive television makes it possible for a great number of individuals to select information tailored to individual motivations and interests. This distinction becomes particularly relevant in the field of health education where information overload has often been identified as a source of unproductive anxiety. By offering, in an interactive environment, a message that is tailored to individual needs and characteristics, this new communications medium closely resembles one-to-one health education methods often recognized as the best approach, but seldom applied because of high costs. For these reasons, interactive television is destined to play an important role as a decision-making support for health-related issues both at the curative and preventive levels.

With regards to treatment, this technology can help doctors, nurses and other professionals in their health education and information tasks by providing a powerful pedagogical tool, the content of which they can define and fashion according to local needs. Through this approach, patients are now able to use often idle time in the waiting room to go through information related to a specific illness or its treatments, in order to be better prepared for their interaction with the medical personnel.

At the same time, this technology constitutes one of the very first pragmatic tools to conduct health education and health promotion programs. Investigators in the field agree that one of the central obstacles to the success of health education campaigns lies in the fact that courses and/or publicity campaigns most often reach the public at times when it is neither receptive nor motivated. In contrast, the presence of a videotex terminal in a health clinic, a hospital, a drugstore, and eventually in the homes, greatly reinforces the probability of easy access to health information at the time and place where this information is needed. For instance, it may very well be at the time of a visit to a doctor for a chronic bronchitis that a patient will be most receptive to information on smoking. In another context, it may very well be when a child has come down with a fever accompanied by skin eruptions that parents will become interested in knowing more about infectious diseases of childhood and the importance of vaccination.

The Tele-Health Project

The Tele-Health service has been launched as a concerted effort to investigate electronic supports to health education. The project is in three parts: creation of a health information videotex databank, operation of an experimental network that is entirely dedicated to health issues, and a series of evaluation studies on the impact of the programs that are available in the Tele-Health bank.

We are presently developing a core content of health education material for the Tele-Health bank. This bank should be augmented further by the participation of interested institutions whose role it is to provide health education services and continuing education services. The public bank, at this time, contains 15 programs of general interest such as nutrition, smoking and alcohol consumption, cardiovascular disease, stress, insomnia, depressive states, infectious diseases in children, vaccination, flu and colds, choosing health care services, and so on. A second part of the Tele-Health databank not accessible to the general public, is aimed at supporting medical practice and continuing medical education.

The databank is made available as an experimental service over a network of 50 terminals located in clinics' and hospitals' waiting rooms, drugstores, and physicians' offices. Serving both demonstration and evaluation purposes, such a flexible exploitation of videotex's potential in the health field should make it possible to identify rapidly the most cost-efficient applications. This comprehensive approach should further guarantee that, in the fast-developing world of videotex implementation, the specifications necessary to develop its potential in the health field will be known from the outset.

Other countries experimenting with Prestel-based services include West Germany, Switzerland, Sweden, Finland, Norway, Austria, the Netherlands, Belgium, and Italy (Tydeman, et al., 1982). Some of the same countries have teletext services running on a fully developed commercial basis. Japan has also experimented with highly sophisticated full-channel teletext services such as HI-OVIS (Highly Interactive Optical Video Information System). Since the Japanese language involves so many characters, it has been difficult to come up with efficient and inexpensive hardware/software. The latest development in Japan is a phone-based system similar to Prestel called Captain (Link, 1983, Tydeman, et al., 1982, Siegel, 1983, Glossbrenner, 1983).

INTERACTIVE CABLE

Related to the videotex technology is two-way cable television. Most new cable systems being installed in the United States have provision for television to be sent to the user and for information to be sent from the user back to the station. In many cases, this two-way system is used to select premium services for which users pay an extra charge, that is, credit-bearing educational programs, adult entertainment, and so on. Using a special decoder box, the viewer can select among regular channels or the pay-per-view variety.

Probably the best-known two-way cable systems are the Warner-Amex Qube systems in Columbus, Ohio; Pittsburgh, Pennsylvania; and Texas. The Columbus system is the company's pioneer market for this technology and has experimented with a number of innovative interactive programs. Using a similar decoder box, viewers can respond to questions posed during a program. Live participants or actors can respond to the audience's aggregate votes. For example, a program about local government services might be presented, and constituents could express their opinions directly to the studio panel. This same voting system has been used to let children "direct" the way in which a children's show would proceed by letting the live actors in the studio know their preferences. An interactive soap opera and game show have also been produced. Of course, in this technology, participants are not really "branched" to different programs; the one program merely responds to the majority vote. Therefore, it must either be live, or selections must be made from a group of prerecorded segments.

Besides accessing special programs and polling, the Qube system can be used for home telemonitoring. Various burglar and fire alarms can be wired into the system, which, when triggered, register at the cable headquarters. In turn, police, rescue, and fire services can be notified. Special services for the homebound, elderly, and handicapped can be incorporated into such a service, all without tying up a phone line.

Because cable systems have the potential for so many channels, many cable franchises have set aside channels for government, education, and social service organizations. If viewers decide that such a service is worth the extra cost and a significant number of homes adopt the technology, there is a great potential for much more participatory community decision-making. In the Qube trials, like most of the other videotex technologies, interest in the system declined quite rapidly, and the interactive programs suffered from having a small and select audience. In many ways, this polling was not much different from the typical call-in program and didn't even allow for as full a response or questioning as the call-in system does. However, by marrying the technologies of full color and motion video with individually selected teletext frames, a more interesting hybrid medium is possible.

SOCIAL, COMMERCIAL, AND LEGAL IMPLICATIONS

> The black bar that rolls down through the television picture and forces you to get up and adjust some little knob on the back of the set—that ugly, unlovable, irritating black line—may turn out to be one of broadcasting's most valuable pieces of undeveloped real estate. The line is the vertical blanking interval, or VBI, and it turns out that [broadcasting] doesn't need most of it anymore. . . . Given the tight fit for satellite transponder time, the VBI represents unused space in a fantastically valuable spot—it's like having a small lot on Manhattan's Fifth Avenue. (DeVries, 1983)

Videotex promises to have significant social, economic, and political effects. As the number of information-based jobs reaches beyond the 50 percent mark, fast access to accurate information will become a crucial element of commercial success. Who will control the information, who will be able to receive it, and what will the effects of widespread telecommunications be?

As information develops as a commodity to be repackaged and marketed, keeping that pipeline accessible to the broad public becomes a major societal concern. Some fear that the upper middle class will become even wealthier because they will have the knowledge tools at their disposal. It is certainly true that current users of videotex services are predominantly high-tech businesses and upscale consumers. In a May 1981 survey of Source customers, it was found that:

> . . . 42% of the users were businessmen, 16% scientists and engineers, 14% computer science workers, and 12% engaged in other professional occupations. Less than 30% belonged to a computer club. The average age of survey respondents was 38, and average annual income was $50,000. (Fifteen percent said they made more than $80,000 annually). Most users were male and held degrees above the baccalaureate level. (Sigel, 1983)

A Day in the Life of Mr. and Ms. Upscale: Proposals for Redirecting New Technologies Toward a Mass Market*

Howard and Terry Upscale live in Keeshberg, Colorado. Terry Upscale is an interior decorator. Howard is a computer salesman and a

*by Donna A. Demac.

successful robotics consultant. Sometime in his career, Howard invented a robot that was so in tune with his wife's needs that when he brought it home and then went away on a business trip, the robot and his wife nearly fell in love.

Their house was constructed around an arboretum approximately fifty years ago. In the 1980's, the Upscale's replaced this with a Home Entertainment and Recuperation Altar. HERA sits on a three-foot-high marble floor.

HERA's components include a big-screen TV; cable system with 68 channels and 4 pay services; stereo unit; home computer panel; two arcade-style video games; videodisc player and self-diagnostic health station. In addition, the Upscales go to HERA to do their banking and shopping and, of course, for relaxation.

Terry and Howard used to fret about wasting energy. They also had moments of wondering how vulnerable HERA was to theft and vandalism. In fact, money regularly disappeared from their bank account. The bank had told them that it could assign a detective to the case but this would have cost a large sum of money.

Computer theft was soon added to environmental pollution, food hazards and toxic wastes in the couple's list of life's sad facts.

One day, Howard and Terry were at home. Terry was in the jacuzzi, video-teleconferencing. She spoke to a neighbor about her recent transaction at the Buyatona clothing videotex boutique.

"I was very fortunate. The computer said to me, 'Terry, this dress will look lovely on you. Before sending it out, I will tack it in at the waist just a bit. Your health chart shows that you lost three pounds last month. We want a perfect fit for that trim figure, don't we now?'"

"Nadine, isn't that the cutest thing?" Terry said.

As she sat in the jacuzzi, Terry was having a complete body x-ray. In addition, television screens on the wall surrounded her with images of unique household objects that she might use in her work.

In another room, Howard was jogging on the electronic treadmill. His walkman headphones with the built-in cordless telephone enabled him to transact business and listen to music as he ran his customary three miles. Then he heard the double beeptone for mail arrival. He went to HERA and found out that his brother, Larry, had wired that he would be paying Howard and Terry a surprise visit that afternoon. HERA's personal note at the end of the message read: Brother is a luddite. Give him HERA's deluxe.

Howard continued running and soon, Larry knocked on the front door.

"Well! What a surprise," Howard said, attempting to sound pleased. "What brings you to see us?"

"It has been more than a year since I heard from you," Larry said. "I dropped by to see how you and Terry are keeping yourselves. I've gotten tired of talking to your machine."

Howard gave his brother something to eat and handed him a booklet about HERA-suntanning. He then went to take a shower.

Five minutes after he stepped into the shower, Howard felt hailstones coming out of the water jets. As he got dressed, he saw Robotsweep dumping the trash from the wastebasket on to the floor. Something was wrong. He stuck his head into the HERA and asked, "Larry, what have you done now?" But it was too late.

The house was going bezerk. Windowshades were racing up and down; lights were blinking wildly; he heard Terry yelling for help. As he raced by the printer into the jacuzzi, he saw paper coming out that read: something very strange. consult instruction book for what to do.

Terry yelled, "I'm burning!" Howard yanked her out of the tub. With Larry in tow, they ran outside. One minute later, HERA groaned and blew the roof skyhigh.

The characters in this story conform to the model of the stereotyped computer and video consumer. They are affluent, keen on toys, energetic and easily fooled—visions of the industry which have yet to be effectively challenged.

The introduction of the new systems has been accompanied by many premature statements about their significance. Yet, in these early stages of experimentation, we are only beginning to understand the changes taking place. It is unfortunate that, by and large, people have received little assistance in exploring possible benefits and risks related to a more electronic existence.

As the story indicates, life in technologyland is not risk-free. At the point of introduction, it is necessary to find out just who a new product was designed for and for what purpose? What will it supplant in relation to one's lifestyle, workplace activity and human relations? The option of slow acceptance should be explored.

Though the Upscales seem to have a penchant for high-tech equipment, they are not oblivious to signs of risk. But safety, they are told, is expensive. Privacy invasion, radiation hazards, and loss of personal control over key elements of one's daily existence have been implicitly downplayed as part of technological progress. Yet such dangers can be checked if there is sufficient investment of resources and the will to find remedies.

Frequently, the hardware vendors depend upon the sureties of American consumer marketing. Videotex and cable channels devoted to selling merchandise will exploit, for example, a woman's worry about appearance, the desire for immortality or a weakness for addictive substances. None of this is totally new. Nevertheless, the old gimmicks should be traced as they move into new markets.

The serious task of discovering community and nonprofit applications for interactive and computerized services awaits wider public attention. Some positive examples have been initiated during the last seven years. At New York University's Interactive Telecommunications Program, a program instructs people in noncommercial applications for hospitals, schools and community organizations. The Office of Communication of the United Church of Christ regularly holds workshops on cable TV and ancillary services.

In addition, in the pursuit of mass markets, corporations are exploring services that would be accessible to people outside the stratum of the upper middle class and large financial institutions.

For example, AgriStar, started in 1982 and developed by AgriData Resources, Milwaukee, is a videotex service for the farmer and rancher. The service, according to the company, will contain more than 10,000 pages of agricultural, business, marketing, commodity, weather and news information. Electronic mail services can also be purchased on the system. The service's average cost per month is estimated at less than $100, with additional equipment-leasing fees added onto overall expenses.

KCET, the Los Angeles public television station, is developing teletext services for two community interest programs. NOW! is KCET's news and information magazine. It contains up-to-the-minute news, in-depth features on community issues, sports scores and other information. The service also offers financial and market information, a guide to L.A. events and the performing arts and a games section. KCET is also experimenting with special reports on topical issues, such as auto safety, health, lifestyle features and background information on legislation before the state and federal governments.

Over the long term, benefits from new systems, serving different sectors of society, will come about through greater public involvement. The most successful applications will be those that are backed by continuous public support. In addition, widespread benefits will very likely depend on some unknown degree of government funding. The government's duty to look out for the nation's welfare today encompasses the very significant impact of computers. An important objective, then, is to see in what ways governmental entities can carry over to computerized systems the expectations regarding low-cost universal benefit from communication technologies that were codified in the Communications Act of 1934.

Creative thinking is needed from the bottom up. Working people, minorities, women and others should be educated about new technologies and encouraged to articulate their needs and interests. Research aimed at balancing market and public requirements, should investigate the least disruptive ways of integrating electronic system inventions into present-day working and home environments.

There is no sin to individual consumption. A pitch, however, to only one set of interests will inevitably result in missed opportunities for the entire society. Moreover, many of the new upscale products may not satisfy even affluent people's appetites and needs. What are the underlying assumptions of those who are marketing the new commodities? Stated otherwise, how good are assumptions that cater only to a mythical gluttonous few? It is quite possible that the Upscales, too, will be aided by a deeper understanding of the risks and benefits to be found in new information technologies.

Another major issue is regulation of the medium itself. How should information be screened? Will advertising copy be subject to regulation? How can we protect consumers when "instant" purchases can be made via videotex? Currently, these issues are covered by a variety of policies and laws, and are dealt with by various commissions, such as the First Amendment, The Federal Trade Commission, and The Federal Communications Commission.

Privacy and security also pose problems in these two-way systems. Since information accessed and transactions made are recorded, how are we to prevent this information from reaching the wrong hands? Who will know what purchases we made this month or what our bank account balances are?

Recently, a movie theater owner in Columbus, Ohio subpoenaed data records of Warner-Amex Cable regarding viewership of a sex-oriented film. The theater owner was being prosecuted for showing obscene films. He wanted to prove that the film met with community approval by citing the fact that many cable subscribers, including a number of prominent citizens, had requested to view the film at home on cable TV. No law prohibited the judge from reviewing and releasing the names of those households that requested the film. As it turned out, he did not. The judge chose only to accept aggregate viewer data to support the case of the theater owner. (Teicher, 1983)

Will videotex provide the technological support for the "electronic cottage"? Many predictions say that home access to data links will allow many job-related functions to be performed in the home or, perhaps, in a community "workstation." This technology may make it easier for homebound persons to hold challenging jobs and for men and women to share jobs and child-rearing. Patterns of housing, work shifts, the nature of jobs, and the employability of the very young and the very old will all come into question when only a given work output and not personal presence define productivity.

WHERE IS THE MEDIUM GOING?

Videotex is a burgeoning medium. The challenge, as in all interactive media, is to find a style that doesn't merely automate traditional textual and graphic presentation but is a uniquely better one. Patterns of videotex usage tend to show a high level of time spent on-line for a few weeks and a very rapid drop-off thereafter. This is especially true of consumers rather than business adopters. This may be because the "novelty" effect wears off, and it simply becomes easier to access the same information in another way (calling a travel agent or reading the newspaper). Perhaps the information or entertainment wasn't so appealing after all.

The standards issue is becoming resolved in many ways. The adoption of the North American standard (NAPLPS) will ease some consumers' minds about having to buy a collection of decoders to access the various systems that will come onto the market (Lax and Olsen, 1983). Cheap decoders are one answer but not the one that many experts predict will make the difference. The real hope for videotex is the already booming personal-computer market. These micros can already receive any ASCII information source, and with simple decoding software or hardware, they can receive NAPLPS or Prestel as well. Since they are already in many homes and offices, they are familiar, and consumers will be anxious to add another feature to them. Additionally, personal computers' memory capability will allow more sophisticated information-sharing and downloading of programs from teletext or videotex.

> For business computing, a major role in software distribution is already passing from computer stores to specialized software-only stores like Microcom. For consumer computing, emerging software distribution channels include full-service computer stores, software-only stores like CBS's Computer Specialty Stores, book and record stores, plus telephone and mail order.
>
> . . . A large number of these programs could be provided over a "Home-PC channel" on cable (or VBI broadcast teletext, DBS, or multichannel MDS). Subscribers would get a monthly "program guide," then download the software they wish to try. (Yankee Group, 1982)

VideoPrint's June 1983 issue said that this new "teledelivery" market will grow from 1983 revenues of $9.1 million to over $20.2 billion in 10 years' time. Of this, about 75 percent will probably result from downloading computer software. Instead of going to the computer store and waiting in line to try out various programs, users could simply download a program from teletext or videotex, and if they like it, save it to disc or tape. It would be much like taping favorite TV shows or music off the air.

This process can be accomplished efficiently by a number of present videotex delivery means. Using a 1200 baud modem, a 32K program could be sent in two to three minutes. Using the vertical blanking interval, the same 32K program would take six seconds to download. Using a full video channel, *200* 32K programs could be loaded in *one second!* (The Yankee Group, 1983)

But cheap, available terminals and fast downloading of programs are only the technical side of making the medium attractive. New styles of writing and frame creation will need to be developed. Human factors will need to receive due attention when designing the database configuration and access methods.

> The earliest human factors research on videotex was conducted with the Prestel system in the U.K. The designers were (quite correctly) concerned that a long system response time would be

disruptive to users. Considerable research has been conducted on the psychological aspects of system response time and the general recommendation is that a response time of less than two seconds is desirable for most operations. However, it is stressed that the variability of response times for a particular operation is more important than the mean response time—i.e. consistency is more critical than absolute speed. (Francas, 1983)

In order for untrained users to be able to access on-line information systems, many use a "menu" approach. Users merely pick from a gradually more specific list of choices until they get to their desired screen or series of screens. This is often called a "tree" approach. While easy to use, it can be time-consuming for experienced users who know exactly which of the thousands of possible topics they want. Most systems, like CompuServe and Source, allow users to either use the menu approach or to enter specific "screen" numbers or names of sections. For instance, while it might take 10 separate menu choices to get to the section in which you can send a piece of electronic mail, if you know the section title or screen number, you can simply type in "MAIL SEND." When searching out topics in banks of articles, however, the task becomes even more complicated, because most often you don't know the name of an article or author for which to search. In such systems, key words can often be entered that search through a list of descriptors or even through an abstract of the article looking for occurrences of the word. By combining key words like "CAI," "EFFECTIVENESS," and "RESEARCH," you can find the articles that contain all those topics.

FIGURE 3-3 Knowledge index search (courtesy of DIALOG Information Services, Inc.).

```
In NEWS2 database:
 S1    27 ARTIFICIAL INTELLIGENCE
 S2     8 COMPUTER SIMULATION

?D 1/M/1-27

1/M/1
2024717
  The computer as translator. (column)
  Pollack, Andrew
  New York Times   v132   p32(N) pD2(L)   April 28   1983
```

Figure 3-3 *(Continued)*

```
CODEN: NYTIA
col 1   015 col in.
illustration; cartoon
EDITION: Thu
1/M/2
2016339
Mind  machines:   can Roger Schank turn a Yale computer
into a
football coach? Simulating patterns in  research,  he
tackles
Aristole-type questions; a program for a president?
Chace, Susan
Wall Street Journal   p1(W) p1(E)   March 30   1983
CODEN: WSJOAF
col 1   050 col in.
illustration; portrait
EDITION: Wed
1/M/3
2016178
Mind  machines:   scientists  are laboring at making
computers
think for theirselves; artificial-intelligence study,
primitive
so far, poses some unnerving issues: awaiting non-vons's
birth.
Chace, Susan
Wall Street Journal   p1(W) p1(E)   March 29   1983
CODEN: WSJOAF
col 1   052 col in.
EDITION: Tue
1/M/4
1987552
A way to talk a computer into running a program.
(Intellect &
other user-friendly natural-language programs)
Aeppel, Timothy
Christian Science Monitor   v75   p13   Feb 17   1983
CODEN: CSMOBF
col 2   002 col in.
EDITION: Thu
GEOGRAPHIC LOCATION: Massachusetts
1/M/5
1987539
```

New electronic information systems will undoubtedly be improved by more powerful accessing functions, helpful comments when errors are made, and, for some special-use terminals, special keyboard design to make interactions simpler.

As on-line systems users employ the medium for conferencing, many new issues arise regarding the changed nature of the communications. Studies were conducted at Carnegie-Mellon University by social psychologists to see how electronic communications shaped decision-making situations.

> "DO NOT BE AN IDIOT. YOU ARE A COMPLETE AND TOTAL IGNORAMUS." These words, typed over a computer terminal during a conversation, are a prime example of "flaming," computerese for an unseemly outburst. When people flame, they send to someone else's terminal sentiments that they would hesitate to express in person. While the person at his keyboards presents one set of problems for psychology, flaming represents the sorts of quirks that arise when people are linked electronically.
>
> . . . The computer sessions [at Carnegie-Mellon] were stormy. It took the groups longer to come to a decision; arguments were common; and the students frequently flamed; they swore, called one another names, and were otherwise abusive. This abuse never occurred when the students talked in person.
>
> But there were pluses for the computer: In person a single, vocal participant sometimes held sway over the group's decision, whereas computer discussions were more equal, everyone getting their share of "air time," and having some weight in the outcome. The computer network, judging from Kiesler's study, suggests a rowdy democracy. (Coleman, 1983)

Whether this response to on-line interactions is a reflection of the novelty of the medium or the age of many computer users is yet to be seen. However, the lack of face-to-face contact certainly yields a different experience. Not unlike citizens band radio, many users of conference and "chat" sections of information utilities assign themselves fanciful "handles" like "Gambler," "Sexy Sally," "Cupcake," and "Secret Spy" (Glossbrenner, 1983). Many corporations are using computer conferencing to cut down on travel time and expenses. Clearly much more experience and research is needed to structure these dialogues so that they are productive and don't lead to awkward interpersonal relationships when electronic correspondents actually meet.

Although [videotex and personal computers] may compete with one another for a while, their products may gradually evolve to the point where they are almost indistinguishable from one another. In the meantime, personal computer owners may benefit from a profusion of powerful graphics products that will become available as a result of this merging. . . . Eventually most of the functions of videotex will be handled by videodiscs, which will be distributed to local cable TV stations and which will display pictures of products as graphically as is now done on TV commercials. (Malloy, 1983)

Several enhancements of the North American videotex NAPLPS standard are now in the works: photographic data transmission, sound (voice or musical tones), animation, and telesoftware that can customize presentations (Lax and Olsen, 1983). Whether videotex and teletext become media unto themselves or emerge as conduits for other media, such as newspaper stories, stock market ticker tapes, CAI programs, video games, and mail, is yet to be seen.

The QUBE Expedition Into the Electronic Future*

Pioneers are a special breed. Their vision casts the future in dimensions beyond the range of ordinary sight. The first QUBE expedition into the electronic future spanned roughly seven years, from 1977 to 1984. The trip encompassed all the thrills and disappointments, the rare discoveries and false starts, of expeditions into more conventional geographies. The peak occurred in 1983 with the launching of the world's first interactive television network. The QUBE Network utilizes satellite technology to beam video signals from Columbus, Ohio into subscriber homes in six QUBE cities: Columbus and Cincinnati in Ohio, Dallas and Houston in Texas, Pittsburgh, Pennsylvania and St. Louis, Missouri. Viewers in the six cities can simultaneously "talk back" to their TV sets by pressing buttons on a handheld console. By "touching in" to respond to questions or services offered, viewers in the six cities transmit digital information through phone data line back to the multicity polling base in Columbus. The first QUBE expedition ended in January of 1984 when the QUBE Network cut back from daily programming to occasional interactive "specials." The economics of cable operations in the Eighties forced major reductions in staff and programming.

*by Carolyn Swift, Ph.D.

In six-plus years of producing interactive shows QUBE staff explored a wide variety of public affairs, sports, entertainment and consumer programming. Along the way we learned a lot about what makes viewers respond to interactive questions. The most effective audience reinforcers—not surprisingly—tap basic human motivations. Monetary incentives draw eighty to ninety percent of the viewing audience to respond. Giving audiences the power to change something also results in a high rate of response. Whether voting to change library hours in their home communities or expressing preferences on a presidential poll, over two-thirds of QUBE audiences characteristically respond to the opportunity to influence events or express opinions on significant issues.

QUBE's interactive programming has produced a long list of television "firsts," some educational, some impacting on community affairs, some entertaining and all creative. Four examples of QUBE "firsts" appear below.

- The first nationally televised interactive poll in response to a Presidential message occurred in July of 1979 when President Jimmy Carter telecast a speech setting forth his national energy policy. Within minutes after his speech QUBE viewers in Columbus were polled about their reactions. The polls and their results were broadcast live on NBC. It was the largest instant electronic public response to date to a Presidential address.

- The first use of interactive television to order products, information and services occurred in 1977 with the initiation of QUBE Service Polls. Responses of individual households to interactive questions are anonymous except for Service Polls, which provide printouts of the viewer information—name and address—needed to deliver the information or service ordered. Viewers are always told, prior to a Service Poll, that their responses to these questions will not be anonymous, but will be identified by household in order to provide the product or service requested. Those wishing to remain anonymous then refrain from touching in. A typical example of this use occurred in Columbus when viewers were given the opportunity to receive a free cosmetic "makeover" at a local department store. The offer generated over 1,500 responses. Those receiving the makeover ended up spending an average of $50 apiece in retail sales. Service Polls have also been used to screen eligible loan applicants. A savings and loan company identified potential borrowers and completed preliminary processing of their loans electronically through Service Polls, thus saving their customers the inconvenience of repeated visits to the lending institution.

- Television's first interactive football game was played in July of 1980. QUBE challenged armchair quarterbacks to match their expertise against professionals by calling the plays in a semipro game. The stadium at Ohio State University was the site for the contest between the Columbus Metros and the Racine Gladiators. In an early play QUBE's living room coaches opted for the "bomb," blitzing the opposition. The long shot paid off and the QUBE team got the first—and its only—score. Heady with success the folks at home stuck with that play too long and ended up losing the game. The show demonstrated that interactive audiences rise to the challenge of being put in charge. Response levels remained high throughout most of the show despite the home team's loss.

• The world's first interactive television drama aired in Columbus in June of 1981. The QUBE audience served as script writer, director and producer for the zany soap opera plot. The storyline followed the heroine, Lulu, from infancy to adulthood. Viewers went for wackiness over logic in deciding Lulu's fate. Starting with the show's title (would you believe "The Chicken Who Ate Columbus"?) they went on to pick Lulu's career, her romantic partner and which Brand X's she put in her grocery cart. The show confirmed the finding that giving audiences the opportunity to be active partners in television viewing inspires a high level of participation. Roughly three-fourths of the viewers influenced Lulu's destiny by answering interactive questions.

What was it like to be part of QUBE's first expedition? Exciting. Challenging. Mind-expanding. Career-stretching. The task now is to integrate interactive applications into solid business plans to lay the groundwork for future QUBE expeditions.

REFERENCES

Aldrich, M., *Videotex: Key to the Wired City* (London: Quiller Press, 1983).

DeVries, T., "Valuable Property in TV Land," *Technology* (August, 1983), p. 70.

Francas, M., "Acceptance of Telidon: Human Factors Issues Deserve Careful Attention," *Videotex Canada* (Summer, 1983), pp. 27-31.

Coleman, D., "The Electronic Rorschach," *Psychology Today* (February, 1983), pp. 36-43.

Glossbrenner, A., *The Complete Handbook of Personal Computer Communications,* (New York: St. Martin's Press, 1983).

Hecht, J., "Information Services Search for Identity," *High Technology* (May, 1983) pp. 58-65.

High Technology, "Business Outlook: Big Gains for Videotex by End of Decade," (May, 1983), p. 66.

Lax, L., and Olsen, M., "NAPLPS Standard Graphics and the Microcomputer," *Byte* (July, 1983), pp. 82-92.

Link Resources Corporation, *Online Database Report* (Volume 4, Number 6), June, 1983.

Link Resources Corporation, *Viewdata/Videotex Report* (Volume 4, Number 6), June, 1983.

Malloy, R., "Commentary: Personal Computers and Videotex," *Byte* (July, 1983), pp. 114-129.

Nora, S., and Minc, A., *The Computerization of Society* (Cambridge, MA: MIT Press, 1980).

Pfister, L., "Teletext . . . Its Time Has Come," speech presented at Videotex '83 Conference, New York, NY, June 28, 1983.

Sigel, E., *The Future of Videotext* (White Plains, NY: Knowledge Industry Publications, 1983).

Teicher, J., "Videotex: The Evolution of A New Mass Medium," unpublished paper, 1983.

Toffler, A, *The Third Wave* (New York: William Morrow and Co., 1980).

Tyler, M., "Videotex, Prestel, and Teletext—The Economics and Politics of Some Electronic Publishing Media," *Telecommunications Policy* (Vol. 3, No. 1), 1979.

Tydeman, J., Lipinski, H., Adler, R., Nyhan, M., and Zwimpfer, L., *Teletext and Videotex in the United States* (New York: McGraw-Hill Publications Company, 1983).

VideoPrints, "Teledelivery Business Quantified: Would You Believe $20 Billion?", June 22, 1983.

Yankee Group, *Yankeevision* (Number 13) February/March, 1983.

CHAPTER FOUR

COMPUTER-ASSISTED INSTRUCTION

Computer-assisted instruction (CAI) has grown out of the developments in both computer hardware and instructional theory. In looking at the phenomenon of CAI, it's important to not only attend to hardware and its constant advancements, but also to the *reasons* for employing it in teaching and informing. Probably most of us are familiar with this new medium through press accounts of the rush to place computers in schools. There are already over 150,000 microcomputers in schools, and some studies predict that there will be one million of them in the schools by the mid-1980s (Kearsley and Hunter, 1983). Over 1.5 million computers are in place in businesses, where they are used partly for training. What are they doing with them, and why the fascination?

"In the beginning," instruction was *all* interactive—person to person. Mentors were able to tailor explanations and practice to the needs and styles of their students. But as mass instruction and the formal classroom became prevalent, it became more and more difficult to individualize instruction. Few students could feel that the pace was really suited to them at any given moment, and they seldom got the chance to actively practice skills or demonstrate their understanding of new material. Group training in industrial, professional, and military settings is often limited in the same ways.

In the 1930s, behavioral psychologists such as B.F. Skinner shifted attention from groups and internal processes to the study of individuals and the external events that characterized their learning. While this research began with simple laboratory situations using animals, some of the basic themes attracted a great deal of interest in education and other forms of training. Simply stated, if you want to introduce new behaviors (1) create a physical setting in which those behaviors (and not others) are going to be the most likely ones—even before you start training; (2) find something that you can do that the individual finds pleasurable each time a step in the right direction is taken; (3) keep those steps small enough so that the rewards are always frequent—even when there are the inevitable ups and downs in performance. Despite the radical nature of these concepts ("Educational practices based on animal training?!" "Give kids rewards for learning!?") they became the inspiration for a new educational mode: programmed instruction.

These lessons were constructed in small steps, each followed by a query. The student immediately responded, and in some way, the correct answer was then revealed. This knowledge of results and eventual praise functioned as the rewards. Early versions of programmed instruction (PI) used printed workbooks in which students could respond in writing to very short questions and then find out the correct answers by revealing parts of a page with an answer key. A slightly more elegant version of this employed "teaching machines" that scrolled forward on correct answers. These early linear PI efforts were often effective in focusing attention on the task at hand and allowing students to work actively at their own pace with some immediate payoff. However, unlike the original one-on-one learning model, where the "instructors" would vary the step size based on the animal-"student's" prior performance, the PI step size was always the same: small. Thus, lessons often became boring. The answer, of course, was to make several versions of the same lesson in small, medium, and large steps and start everyone at the medium size. The questions would make you respond actively, give you some feedback, but also branch you to the step size you apparently needed at that point. Great, but who does the branching? Some early branching PI used "scrambled books" that send people to different pages based on their responses. But the ultimate "branching device" was still getting its act together.

During the 1960s, the computer evolved from a huge device that turned batches of punched cards into payrolls and address labels into the center for a network of interactive terminals, making a number of simultaneous "conversations" possible. The computer had become a branching teaching machine. Manufacturers began experimenting with using computers to deliver instruction. Some of the early projects that had major impacts on this field were Control Data Corporation's PLATO system, the Mitre Corporation's TICCIT system (now owned by Hazeltine), and the IBM 1500 system. In the next two decades, millions were spent on research and development by both private industry and the government. The PLATO system was based on a specially designed graphics terminal that could show slides, play music, and respond to touch. Using a mainframe computer at the University of Illinois, users could access the system over phone lines. This pioneering project developed Tutor, a special computer language oriented toward instructors writing their own courses. These could then be shared by others throughout the world. TICCIT used a large computer installed in each location that could "drive" terminals around a campus. This system also had the capability of accessing videotaped programs to be interspersed with CAI lessons. A major instructional advance of TICCIT was its framework of instruction, in which learners could call up examples, rules, exercises, course objectives, and so on, according to their own preferences and learning styles. Although forms of the PLATO and TICCIT systems are in use today, at the time they were introduced they proved unwieldy for widespread use. However, they spawned many of today's leaders in microcomputer instruction and interactive video.

Early experiments with large mainframes proved the potential utility of CAI, but it was not until there were faster, stand-alone, and cheaper computers and authoring languages for standard computer systems that CAI became a real instructional force. These first CAI efforts were expensive and were not fully supported by teachers for a variety of reasons:

> When a good message isn't communicated, we usually find fault with the sender or the channel through which it is passed. In the case of computer-aided instruction, the computerists have blamed it on "threatened" teachers. The teachers meekly shouldered the "obstructionist" label. What they should have said was that early computer-aided instruction was dull for most students and really didn't attempt a sufficient range of human-oriented challenges. The teachers should have been assertive enough to reply that computerists were too pompous and self-involved to create truly motivating and interesting instruction. But perhaps teachers were intimidated by the science/computer priesthoods of the 1960s and 1970s and merely obstructed rather than demanded better programs. The result was failure for the computers and a certain deprivation for the students.
>
> ... The Space Invaders are trying to tell us not just what games should be, but what all education should be and perhaps what all man-machine interface should be. With the micro-computer revolution, a few creative programmers realized what ordinary folks wanted from *any* interaction, live, print, or whatever ... and what they weren't getting. So the Space Invaders are trying to tell the teachers and the managers something that most people under 20 know already: One-way information is a bummer. (Hon, 1981)

Now that we have relatively simple, inexpensive, portable personal computers, we no longer need special facilities or princely bankrolls to be able to use one. Most five-year-olds can get a "micro" up and running—a feat worthy of a team of high-priced engineers only as long ago as the 1970s. No longer are dozens of users "down" because the main frame "crashes"; if a micro goes down, the user can simply move to a new machine. Finally, we're starting to have access to competent CAI lessons, because one no longer needs a computer science degree or even the knowledge of a relatively simple language like BASIC to program a lesson. Of course, those organizations with large mainframe or minicomputers already on hand can and are using them for informational and instructional programs as well as the large-scale data processing applications.

The advantages of CAI? As we have seen, learners can go at their own pace, not the "average" pace of the class. The computer can present material, quiz the user, and, depending upon the answer, "branch," or go to an appropriate lesson segment explaining why an answer was wrong or jump ahead to the next concept. Instead of passively reading or listening, a CAI user must actively respond to a lesson, leading to greater retention (Schramm, 1977). But beyond branching instruction, the computer can simulate events too dangerous, complex, or expensive to be done in the real world. For instance, medical students can experiment with various treatments and drug dosages on a computer-simulated patient without the risk of failure and personal harm. Music, sound effects, and graphics (complete with animation) just like you see on video games can be incorporated into a lesson, giving more ways to express concepts. Finally, the computer is a great record keeper, retaining student responses, scores, class averages, and so on.

Like a lot of interactive media, the use of computers for instructional purposes goes by a number of names. When computers are used to *deliver* the instruction, it's known as CAI, or computer-assisted instruction—or CAL for computer-assisted learning. Another shorthand is CBI for computer-based instruction, or CBT for computer-based training. Computers can also be used to *manage* learning activities, such as scheduling classes, recording student grades and courses completed, and budgeting training activities. This application is known as CMI: computer-managed instruction. For instance, many corporations keep track of which training sessions employees have attended or will need to attend, budget their travel and per diem allowances for attending courses off-site, and record testing data to be used in later promotions, raises, or, in the case of safety training courses, for insurance purposes. For instance, Boeing Aerospace Company in Seattle uses CMI for training forecasts, schedules, tracking of training requests, schedules for instructors and classes, time changes, budgets, course indexes, course descriptions, and statistics of student activity (Clogston, 1980). But all these acronyms have a lot in common (we'll stick with CAI).

CAI includes a variety of forms and styles. Some of the most common are drill and practice, tutorial, tailored information, and even beyond instruction to simulation. For instance, elementary school students can get tireless coaching in spelling and arithmetic through CAI. While this form is valuable, its overuse has stereotyped it as CAI. These kinds of programs need not be limited to the "flash card" type format: one popular typing program lets you shoot down alien battleships if you type in a word correctly and rapidly enough. If you're a bad typist, watch out! Heliflight Systems of Conroe, Texas uses CAI to help foreign helicopter pilots learn English vocabulary and

FIGURE 4-1   Figures 4-1 through 4-3 show screens from the Stickybear CAI series (courtesy of Optimum Resources, Inc.).

FIGURE 4-2

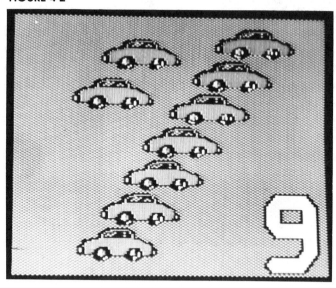

FIGURE 4-3

grammar, while not tying up human trainers with repetitious drills (Quy and Covington, 1982).

Tutorials lead the learner through information in a dialogue format. This style makes ample use of branching based on the correctness of responses, but it may also do so in response to a student's overall style or performance, by a stated preference for content or sequence through menus. Tutorials often present graphics: charts, diagrams, and illustrations to aid in the explanation of technical material. Alfred Bork, at the University of California, Irvine, has been responsible for the development of several CAI concepts and programs, including tutorials in physics. Not only can graphics be used to illustrate complex technical concepts, but students can build graphics interactively, using their own formulas and inputs. Through the changing visual patterns, students can more readily interrelate the abstract and the concrete.

Lest we stereotype CAI as a schoolroom phenomenon, its largest area of growth seems to be in business and industry. Tuscon's Pima Community College and Mountain Bell have cooperatively produced CAI to train telephone installers. The Customer Equipment Service Division of Eastman Kodak uses Apple computers to teach repair procedures for equipment such as large copiers (Quy and Covington, 1982). Efficiency, in terms of cost and time, is the largest reason for CAI's acceptance in the industrial world. In a 1981 article in the magazine published by the American Society for Training and Development, Ben Graves of the Olin Corporation in Stamford, Connecticut commented on the medium's successes. "Formerly, it took new customer service representatives from three to six months to reach 80 percent efficiency. Now they reach that same level of proficiency in four to five weeks." Olin uses the IBM IIS (Interactive Instruction System) to deliver training on the same terminals many employees use to perform their daily jobs. (*Training and Development Journal*, 1981). Xerox Corporations's Administrative Training Department reports that CAI cut costs of training from $33.00 per student hour for "live" training to $8.28 per student hour by eliminating the need to travel to the training center in Leesburg, Virginia. (Wolman, 1982).

Computers Teach People About Computers*

A training class is being conducted at a major manufacturing corporation. Let's eavesdrop . . .

Teacher: Hello! What's your name?

Student: Michael.

Teacher: Hi Michael. Today we're going to look at order processing. Here's a list of topics. Where would you like to begin?

Student: I think I'd like to learn about order entry.

Teacher: Fine. Entering customer orders requires the use of several procedures. Let's take a look at them. . .

The lesson is one of a series of customer service courses instructing company reps in such areas as order entry, order processing, adding customers, deleting customers, etc.

The training classes are held frequently and at times, round the clock. Sessions are often conducted in California, New York, and Iowa at the same time. That's because the "teacher" conversing with Michael is a computer!

Michael is one of many students who learns his job skills via computers. Computer-assisted instruction incorporates several instructional methodologies:

- Simulation: Screens resembling on-line production screens provide a "test system" into which the student enters sample order information. Function keys are assigned paging and processing functions, letting the student move from screen to screen or press the proper key as if actually processing an order.
- Tutorial: Text screens can outline procedures, present concepts, and illustrate "forms" on the screen, highlighting each required entry. Various question formats provide opportunities to test the learner, tailoring subsequent reviews and remediation to learners who require them.
- Drill and practice: Using the simulated screens (e.g. order entry screens), the learner enters practice orders over and over until s/he enters each field correctly.

The ability to provide "simulation," "tutorials," and/or "drill and practice" exercises are the "pros" typically associated with CAI. However, there is perhaps a greater asset to the use of CAI in teaching

*by Lynn Hessinger.

computer skills—it familiarizes learners with the computer and keyboard itself.

Many of today's job fields—customer service, banking, accounting and finance, to name a few—increasingly rely on computers for information storage and retrieval. Many older employees have had little or no personal exposure to computers, yet they see them everywhere—in homes, schools, offices—and will probably walk in to work one day to find a computer at their own work stations!! First-time users are often frightened and apprehensive, afraid that they might "break" the computer or "mess up" the "stuff" inside.

Many CAI lessons can be taken on the same terminal that the learner will use every day to perform the actual job task(s). Thus, CAI presents two levels of instruction:

- The obvious level is the course itself. For example, CAI can teach an employee how to input data and to correct possible entry errors.
- The second ("hidden") level teaches the employee how to use the keyboard, press the "Enter" key, and move from screen to screen.

Without realizing it, learners who complete a course in customer service have also completed a course in basic computer skills and orientation. The key result: familiarity with the computer and a subsequent reduction of user fears and anxieties.

This point was evidenced in a course series conducted for data entry personnel at a major multinational corporation:

Traditionally, employees were flown in to company headquarters for a week of lectures and "terminal" exercises covering 30 to 40 different personnel transaction screens. The screens were initially presented by a series of overhead transparencies with accompanying student workbooks. After the lectures, the students were paired at computer terminals to practice entry exercises for each transaction. Most teams spent the major part of the practice sessions encouraging one another to "be the first" to sit down at the keyboard/monitor—neither team member wanted that responsibility!

Another training series was conducted after several CAI courses covering seven major transaction screens had been developed. This time, learners met at headquarters for a 3-day training session. The prerequisite: the CAI courses.

When the trainees arrived, they were impatient. They wanted to see the actual computer screens, not transparencies of them. In fact, a few of them had coerced fellow employees at their "home sites" to let them look at the transaction screens that weren't covered in the initial courses to familiarize themselves before attending the lecture—quite a difference from the first group. These folks couldn't wait for the computer exercises and, in fact, finished the training in two days, managing to get third day off to attend a Broadway play in New York.

The course series is now complete and employees sign up for the courses whenever and wherever they need them. The corporation is saving dollars in travel and live instructor expenses, but the major bonus is the one that is frequently overlooked when considering CAI: The reduction of user fears and anxieties!

Some examples of courses that I've developed include:

- A course that instructs industrial hygienists how to complete a sampling form used when monitoring employee exposure to possible contaminants in the work environment.
- A series of data entry courses for a human resource personnel/payroll system.
- A series of courses to teach a language used to obtain reports from a database.

All of the courses I mentioned are taken by learners across the nation— anywhere that a terminal is available. The courses therefore reach many employees in many divisions regardless of geographical location. This saves the corporations travel monies and expenses and provides available training any time it is needed.

Another genre of CAI might be termed "interactive information." Unlike the stereotypic classroom use of computer-based tutorials or drills, interactive information systems are more like an on-call data bank. For instance, computer systems have been set up in shopping malls to provide suggestions about what to buy friends and family for the holidays. A person can enter the sex, relationship (mother, father, brother, and so on), and price range and get a list of gift ideas and at what stores they can be purchased. Similar setups in hotels, stations, or airports give tourist information such as restaurant guides, public transportation schedules, and local events. Users can access data by choosing a category from a menu, typing in a word or phrase, pressing coded buttons, or even touching the area of interest on a screen.

Responsive instruction has been the goal of good teaching, but many educators have also emphasized the need for people to learn under their own control or "discover" concepts as part of the classroom experience. Discovery learning requires a great deal of interactive skill to manage a situation so that there is the right blend of the known and unknown to maintain an attractive challenge. The computer really shines as a creator of discovery situations.

> Another possibility is to present an investigative facility or interactive world for student use. In such an environment students can explore freely, gaining experiences that may not normally be available in any other way. Such a world can be used either freely or as part of an author—structured experience, perhaps a controlled experiment with the computer showing what the student is doing and offering advice where appropriate.
>
> . . . One of the principal values of the interactive world dialog is that it provides the possibility of building up student intuition and insight into the way things behave, often by providing a wide range of experiences to the student. Such intuition is an important aspect of learning, and one that is often difficult to accomplish within the traditional course.
>
> We are often criticized for producing students who know how to carry out the mathematical manipulations in Science courses, but who are unable to intuit beyond the formal derivations. So dialogs providing experience are useful. (Bork, 1981)

One important category of these interactive miniworlds are simulations such as the popular Apple computer program called Lemonade Stand. It is actually an example of a business simulation, although accessible to "children" of all ages. The user is in charge of running a lemonade stand; lemons, sugar, and glasses must be purchased depending upon the anticipated demand. To manipulate this demand, you may choose to put up some signs advertising your new enterprise—but they cost, of course. And then, sometimes the price of raw materials goes up, and your mother wants you to pay a bit more for your ingredients. To further complicate the matter, the weather and competition change each day. You've got to figure out how much to spend on materials, how much lemonade to make, and how much advertising to buy. If you're a savvy entrepreneur, you can wind up making a good bundle.

Even though this seems like a simple situation, it includes all the elements of a good simulation: realistic content and processes, including some unpredictability. Computer-based simulations have been developed for a variety of medical, economic, interpersonal, and mechanical processes.

An interest in the discovery approach to teaching mathematics to children led Seymour Papert to go a step beyond simulation in the development of LOGO. This special-purpose language created a learning environment in which even very young children can try out their ideas in simple geometry and learn by seeing their results. In addition, following some of Jean Piaget's concepts, LOGO can begin working in the young child's terms of numbers: bodily movement, and then become more abstract in steps. The child's stand-in is a turtle, which the miniprogrammer directs. Some instructions are not "understood" by the turtle, while others produce unexpected results. Like putting a puzzle together, the goal is not at all error-free performance but solving the problem. The computer's consistent and patient response to the inevitable errors make it an ideal context for discovery learning.

> In many schools today, the phrase "computer-aided instruction" means making the computer teach the child. One might say the *computer is being used to program* the child. In my vision, *the child programs the computer,* and in doing so, both acquires a sense of mastery over a piece of the most modern and powerful technology and establishes an intimate contact with some of the deepest ideas from science, from mathematics, and from the art of intellectual model building. (Papert, 1980)

Using English words, the "robot" turtle is moved about on the floor. For older children (as soon as they are ready), the turtle becomes a triangle on the screen that can move and draw lines and shapes; finally, the child may opt for the turtle to disappear, and "imagine" the turtle's relative positions and figure out how to give it proper instructions. LOGO is an example of a *recursive,* or "smart," program that can "learn" new commands from the child. For example, here a child gives the turtle instructions on how to draw a box. He defined a new procedure he calls "box" by using LOGO built-in commands, or "primitives." Thereafter, in that program the language recognizes "box" as a command just like a built-in one. Then "box" is used to define the figure he decided to call "pinwheel."

```
TO BOX
FORWARD 40
RIGHT 90
FORWARD 20
RIGHT 90
FORWARD 40
RIGHT 90
FORWARD 20
END

TO PINWHEEL(RIGHT 45 BOX)
RIGHT 180
FORWARD 50
END
```

(Abelson, 1982)

Whether through traditional CAI, simulation, or LOGO and similar languages such as SMALLTALK, active, creative learning is being supported through interactive technology. Schools across the world are allowing young children to develop important programming and strategy skills that can be applied to computers as well as to other problems, often with surprising and far-reaching results.

WHAT'S IT LIKE TO LEARN WITH CAI?

Admittedly, the thought of learning from a hard, cold machine instead of a real human being might seem a bit undesirable. Many of us have had unfortunate experiences with computers reacting in the stereotypic "does not compute" fashion. Actually, we can design CAI to be more consistently *humane* than we ourselves might be instructing in a traditional school or industrial classroom.

When we think about it, how much does the average lecture really rely on human-to-human interaction? In many classes, most of the individual's time is spent listening to an instructor lecture and others students replying. Even in the best of lectures, some information is redundant, and some is confusing to any one of us. Through CAI, individuals can learn at their own pace. A well-designed program can respond meaningfully to errors more consistently than many people can. Of course, it's not the *computer program,* it's the *programs author* interacting with the student.

Let's take a look at what an instructional interaction is like. Here's an example of a CAI tutorial on the topic of CAI and how the program responds to two different users.

```
In this program, you'll learn the basic principles and practices
of CAI.   But first, what's your name?

>Diane

Hi, Diane! And in a word, what's your occupation?

>teacher

Interesting. . .lots of teachers seem to be getting interested in
computers. But just one more question: you're interested in using
computers to. . .

>teach my students media budgeting skills

Good.   Then we'll work on a program to teach your students media
budgeting skills.   Ready?


In this program, you'll learn the basic principles and practices
of CAI.   But first, what's your name?

>larry

Hi, Larry! And in a word, what's your occupation?

>videography

Interesting. . .lots of people in videography seem to be getting
interested in computers. But just one more question: you're
interested in using computers to. . .

>teach the commercial production staff about new financing plans

Good, then we'll work on a program to teach the commercial
production staff about new financing plans.   Ready?
(OmniCom Associates, 1982)
```

In that example, the computer was echoing the individuals' interests by "remembering" their responses, doing a bit of analysis, and using their own phrases to introduce the theme of the program. As you can see, the computer can do a bit of response editing. The second user, Larry, didn't capitalize the first letter in his name on the computer. However, the program was designed to automatically capitalize the first letter in the variable in which the name was stored. Notice how the computer handles their occupation. The first person said "teacher," and the program somehow knew just to add an "s" to that word to say that "lots of *teachers* are interested in computers." In the second example, the person said "videography"; however, that word wouldn't sound right if put into the sentence, "lots of *videographys.* . . ."

Behind this "intelligent" response is the basic process of all CAI. The computer analyzes the participant's response and matches it against a *template,* or key, that the author has created. That's the only way the computer can "know" how to respond, whether it's in regard to phrasing a response or deciding whether an answer was correct or incorrect. Being able to respond to a range of student input is what makes a program truly "interactive," and the key to that process is a lot of analysis and hard work on the part of the program author.

Let's look at another interaction. In this example, the program presents a case study of an organization looking into automating their list of clients and prospects. After the student has learned about micro-, mini-, and mainframe computers, he or she must decide what to recommend for this organization. The correct answer happens to be a microcomputer. But if the learner types in "minicomputer", the program branches to a series of smaller "frames," or teaching segments:

```
So you'd recommend a minicomputer.  Do you remember how many "K"
or kilobytes, a minicomputer usually has?

>sure

How many?

>48

Actually, a minicomputer usually has at least around 256K.  Do you
think that is more or less than a microcomputer?

>more

Right.  Microcomputers usually have from 4 to 128K.  Do you think
that would be sufficient for the job described?

>no way

Perhaps you were confused by the requirement that the computer be
able to handle up to 1,000 names and records of clients. However,
it isn't necessary to store all that information at once in the
computer's memory. . .
```

In this example, the CAI program was able to diagnose exactly where the learner's confusion was. A person who answered "minicomputer" might have become confused and thought it was smaller than a micro, but by asking some questions, that was ruled out. The learner's misconception was in dealing with the concepts of memory and access to record storage, and the program was able to address that fact. Certainly, this goes far beyond merely telling someone they are "right" or "wrong"; good CAI programs can give feedback that's appropriate to the learner on a minute-by-minute basis.

Simulations can be some of the most engaging kinds of learning experiences. Rather than merely stepping through a program once and being done with it, a student can run through a simulation a number of times, trying different strategies or numerical values. Through this, they can practice rules they have already been exposed to, or they can inductively learn new rules. An example of this kind of program is one that explores the effects of certain drugs on a turtle's heart. Experiments that are commonly done on laboratory animals can be conducted through computer simulation, saving animals' lives, time, and money, and allowing each student to explore many more combinations of treatments. The experiment is graphically depicted by a green turtle, a hypodermic needle that can be filled up with various drugs displayed on a menu, and some general command or information text lines. The hypodermic needle is filled by selecting a drug, typing in its name, and then turning the paddles on the computer that control the amount. As you turn the paddles, colored liquid appears to fill the hypodermic. To administer the drug, you press one of the paddle buttons. The turtle's heart rhythm is displayed by a moving graphic of waves as they would be seen on an electrocardiograph read-out. If you kill the turtle, it turns over on its back, and you can try again.

HOW ARE CAI PROGRAMS DEVELOPED?

Typical CAI programs are created by typing into a computer the text that you want to appear and commands for drawing and displaying graphics, accepting answers, analyzing input, and branching to subprograms based on response analysis. These commands can be written using a standard computer language such as BASIC or Pascal, or by using *authoring languages* or *authoring systems*. All-purpose programming languages may not contain commands for frequently performed functions in a particular area like CAI. On the other hand, there may be a number of unneeded ones. For writing CAI lessons, specialized languages and systems for authors have been developed. "A large part of the reason that there is such a shortage of CAI courseware at this time is that it is so costly in time and money to produce CAI courseware for the CAI models that prevail today. Estimates vary as to the cost, but a ratio of two hundred hours to produce, field-test, and validate a one-hour lesson segment is not uncommon" (Burke, 1982).

FIGURE 4-4 Example of a program listing written in Apple SuperPILOT (courtesy of OmniCom Associates).

```
t:
t:Its purpose is to provide you with a
:basic understanding of some important
:concepts and terminology related to
:the stock market.
as:
g:es
t:What's your first name?
t: (type it in, then press RETURN)
T:
TH:
a:$n$
c:/n$ c
g:es
t:OK, $n$ , have you ever invested in
:stocks?
th:
a:
mj:%ye!sure!defin!%y%!of&course!once!ti
:me!you&bet
jy:know
mj:%no!don&know!never!%n%!don&think!
jy:expl
m:*
jy:huh
```

FIGURE 4-4 *(Continued)*

```
*know
g:v
g:es
t:
t:
t:
t:
t:GOOD.....Then let's jump over some of
:the basic explanation and see how much
:you already know!
w:4
j:table
*huh
g:v
g:es
t:
t:
t:I'm really not sure how to interpret
:what you typed in....but let's look at
:some information about the stock
:market, OK?
W:3
J:expl
*expl
g:v
g:es
t:More than 32 million Americans own
:stocks, bonds, or other types of
:securities.  Investing in these can be
:an interesting and profitable
:experience, but it CAN become a bit
:complicated.
w:4
t:
t:Let's look at some of the different
:kinds of securities .... what they
:are, and their advantages and
:disadvantages.
as:
g:es
t:
t:****COMMON STOCKS ****
```

FIGURE 4-4 *(Continued)*

```
T:
T:  When you buy a share of common
:stock in a
:company, you become a part owner of
:that company.  In order to raise
:money, a company sells stocks - or
:little pieces of "control" in the
:company.
w:4
t:
t:Depending upon how the
:company is doing, shares of stock may
:go up or down in price.
w:3
t:
t:You can earn money in two ways:
t:
t:  first, by selling your stock for a
:price higher than you paid for it;
t:
t:  secondly, by holding onto your
:common stock, and receiving DIVIDENDS.  If
:the company is doing well, you get
:payments - sort of like interest -
:according to how many shares you hold.
as:
*q1
g:es
t:Now, $n$ , what do we call those
:payments given to shareholders when a
th:company is doing well?
a:
m:dividend
t:
ty:RIGHT!
tn:A DIVIDEND is the payment distributed
:to shareholders.
w:3
t:
t:...and what kind of stock pays
th:variable dividends?
a:
```

FIGURE 4-4 *(Continued)*

```
m:common
t:
ty:
:PERFECT!
tn:
: it's called COMMON STOCK.
as:
g:es
t:****PREFERRED STOCK****
T:
T:Preferred stock is also a share of
:ownership in a company.  However,
:unlike COMMON stock, preferred
:stockholders do NOT have a voice in a
:company's management.
w:4
t:
t:Preferred stocks have a SET rather
:than variable dividend which doesn't
:go up or down depending upon how the
:company is doing.
w:4
t:
t:A company must pay the set dividend
:on preferred stocks BEFORE they can
:pay dividends on any common stock.
as:
g:es
*q2
t:Which kind of stock do you think is
:LESS speculative - common or
th:preferred?
a:
m:preferred!PREFERRED
t:
ty:That's right -
tn:NO -
w:2
t:
t:- because preferred
:stock pays set dividends which must be
:paid out before any common stock
```

FIGURE 4-4 *(Continued)*

```
:dividends can be offered.
as:
j(n=2):fini
c:n=2
*table
g:es
g:v0,39,1,10
t:STOCK TABLE
t:
t:------------------------------------
t:high  low    stock &    yield p/e
T:              ` div in $     %
t:------------------------------------
t: 42    27 1/4  XYZ co.2    5    10
t:------------------------------------
t:------------------------------------

g:v0,39,11,23
t:Looking at the chart above, how much
:do you think XYZ stock sold for at its
:highest?
a:
t:
m:42
ty:RIGHT
tn:No, look under the first column.  See
:where it says "high"? The 42 here
:indicates that during the past year,
:XYZ sold for $42.00 a share at its
:highest.
as:
g:es
t:27 1/4, then indicates how much the
th:stock sold at its...
a:
t:
m:low!worst
ty:Correct! At its lowest, it sold for
:$27.25, in the charts represented as
:27 1/4.

tn:27 1/4 or $27.25 is the lowest the
:stock sold for during the past year.
```

FIGURE 4-4 *(Continued)*

```
as:
g:es
t:Under the column "stock and div. in
:$," the XYZ Co. 2 indicates that XYZ's
:last annual dividend amount is $2 per share.
t:The next column, "yield" indicates
:that $2 per year is a 5% yield.
as:
g:es
t:P/E stands for price/earnings ratio.
:The number 10 indicates that the
:earnings for the past year were about
:$4.00.
as:
g:v
g:es
t:sales    high    low    close   net
t:in 100s                        change
t:-----------------------------------
t:  61    40 1/4  39 1/2  40     +1/4
t:-----------------------------------
t:-----------------------------------
t:
g:v0,39,11,23
t:Reading across the table further, we
:have this data.  How many shares do
:you think were traded last year?
a:
mj:6100!61&hundred
jy:r
mj:61
jy:h
m:*
jy:w
*r
t:
t:Right!
as:
j:daily
*h
t:
t:You've got the idea, but add on the
```

FIGURE 4-4 (Continued)

```
:zeros!  There were 6100 shares traded
:last year.
as:
j:daily
*w
t:
t:There were 6100 shares traded last
:year.  Multiply the number under
:"sales in 100s" by 100.
as:
j:daily
*daily
g:es
t:The high price for the day listed
:here is $40.25.  1/4 means 25 cents.
t:
t:So, what was the low for the day?
t:
a:
m:39 1/2!39.50
ty:You've got it.
tn:The low was $39.50.
as:
g:es
t:At closing, how much did the stock
:cost per share?
t:
a:
m:$40!40.!40&dollars!forty
ty:Right .... $40.00
tn:It cost $40.00.
as:
g:es
t:Finally, $n$ ,look at the last
:column.  Do you think the price went
:up or down?
t:
a:
m:up!higher!+
ty:Right, it went up 25 cents per share
:over the preceding day.
tn:No, it went up 25 cents per share
```

FIGURE 4-4 *(Continued)*

```
:over the preceding day.
as:
g:es
t:Considering all the information we've
:seen on this stock, would you think
:it's a COMMON stock or a PREFERRED
:STOCK?
T:
a:
m:common
jy:s
jn:back
*s
t:Sure, because the dividend changes
:periodically.
as:
j:fini
*back
t:It's a common stock, because
:the dividend of this stock
:varies. Perhaps you should go over
:some information on common and
:preferred stocks again.
as:
j:expl
*fini
g:v
g:es
gx:chart
g:v0,39,11,23
t:Hope you've found this brief
:introduction to stocks helpful.
t:
t:Happy investing!
s:32,10;44,10;56,10
w:2
l:hello

e:
```

Authoring languages require that the writer learn some basic codes for CAI functions; however, each code might represent a number of commands in the all-purpose language, and the codes are usually *mnemonic* for their functions: "T" means the words following the "T" will be "Typed" onto the screen, and "M" means check to see if the answer "Matches" a key word or phrase in PILOT. Authoring systems are even easier to learn. By answering simple English questions, or "prompts," on the screen, a course author can create a lesson. One can simply select from a menu to write a "text screen," or a "multiple-choice question screen," and so on. Authoring systems "cookbook" the programming process. However, the tradeoff of this ease is a certain rigidity in the lesson design. Obviously, a simple menu cannot cover the myriad ways in which an author might want to construct a sequence. Often, authoring systems put up stock phrases within a lesson. You don't have to type them in, but the student might get awfully tired of seeing the phrase "CORRECT. GO ON TO THE NEXT ITEM." each time he or she answers something correctly. Furthermore, it may actually take longer for an experienced lesson designer to program using an authoring system than an authoring language. To avoid the use of non-English codes, authoring systems prompt the programmer by asking a series of questions. With some systems, after a while authoring a program can seem like playing "20 questions" (Williams and Gayeski, 1982).

FIGURE 4-5 Example of how a multiple-choice question is created using I.De.A.S., an authoring system (courtesy of OmniCom Associates).

```
This is an example of a(n)
    1 authoring language
    2 programming language
    3 authoring system

Type your answer here -> /

Score this item? y
How many alternatives ? 3
```

FIGURE 4-5 *(Continued)*

```
Alternative   1 branches to screen? 4
     and earns how many points? 0
Alternative   2 branches to screen? 5
     and earns how many points? 0
Alternative   3 branches to screen? 6
     and earns how many points? 100
Is all of the above correct (Y or N)? y


        This is screen 3
```

Authoring languages and programs often work on only one particular machine because they are built for specific functions and keyboards. For instance, computers vary in terms of memory, graphics capabilities, and music generators. Programs written on one microcomputer cannot necessarily be directly "played back" on another brand. This can create some problems for developers who want to share or market their CAI.

Being a good computer programmer doesn't necessarily mean you'll be a good CAI developer, or vice versa. The keys to effective interactivity are good communications and teaching skills. In order to create a program that will respond intelligently to users' input, a course author must already have access to all the likely answers to questions and program in a response to them. What are synonyms or colloquialisms that should be considered? How should misspellings be handled? Capitalizations? Nothing can spoil the feeling of interactivity more quickly than a program that judges an answer wrong when the user merely typed in an acceptable synonym.

Simulations are even more challenging to create. First, a mathematical or conceptual model must be developed. For instance, say you wanted to create a simulation on how to budget for an addition to a house. First, you'd have to consider all the parameters in terms of cost: size, materials, who will do the job, geographic area, length of time. Then you'd have to consider skill levels of the person(s) doing the work and what time deadlines are required. Finally, you'd have to decide how all those factors interrelated and come up with formulas that express those relationships. Only when you had developed a real model that worked out in terms of actual cases could you even begin to program.

> There is something infectious about working with microcomputers. Almost everyone who works with them is won over. Even people who were reluctant, fearful, resentful, or even hostile at first seem to quickly grow fond of their micros.
>
> . . . For purposes of comparison, it seems to me that only 10 percent of what makes a good CAI author has anything to do with computers or computer knowledge. The remainder has to do with a knowledge of how people learn and with creativity. To me, creating CAI is more like writing poetry than it is like anything else. In both CAI and poetry, one has to appreciate the importance of using words in ways that achieve specific results. One must have the creativity to think up options and the endurance to perservere and keep writing and rewriting until the desired result is obtained. (Burke, 1982)

Just because the computer can be an effective teaching tool doesn't mean it will be appropriate in all cases. Long stretches of text can be more easily read from a book than off a screen. Some concepts need realistic pictures, motion, and/or sound to be conveyed. However, CAI is extremely effective for topics and audiences for which the branching and computing capabilities can be exploited. When learners vary greatly in styles, speed, or knowledge of the content, CAI can present information in a much more tailored and relevant manner. When presenting concepts that require mathematical manipulation, the computer can do that quickly, and even interactively display charts or graphs based on user input. It is easy to record responses on disc, tape, or paper so that the course author or instructor can see exactly *what* trainees are thinking and responding. Unlike other kinds of instruction and information, this medium provides for built-in feedback that can be used for fine-tuning the program. For instance, if the author finds that one question is constantly being missed, he or she might go back and look over the explanation of that material to see how it might be presented more clearly. In a tailored information system, organizations might find out what kinds of products or services potential customers are most interested in.

Milner and Wildberger (1974) constructed the following "continuum of instructional uses of computers":

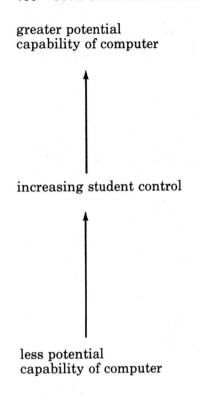

greater potential
capability of computer

increasing student control

less potential
capability of computer

Student-designed automation

Student-developed simulations of real systems or processes

"Opened-ended" problem-solving (student solution of complex and/or student-posed problems)

Student-programmed automata

Student-developed instruction (e.g., tutorials)

Exploration of simulated systems or environments (computer simulated experiments)

Interactive information retrieval

Generative CAI; multilevel branching; artificial intelligence applications

Instructional management systems

Calculation (electronic slide rule)

Tutorial (computerized programmed instruction, or "multiple choice" CAI)

Testing and record keeping

Drill and practice

WHERE IS CAI GOING?

Will the instructional use of computers have the impact its proponents hope for? Is CAI as effective as some studies seem to demonstrate? If so, where will the money for the equipment come from?

Let's consider the cohort of children who will enter kindergarten in the year 1987, the "Class of 2000," and let's do some arithmetic. The direct public cost of schooling a child for 13 years, from kindergarten through 12th grade is over $20,000 today (and for the class of 2000, it may be closer to $30,000). A conservatively high estimate of the cost of supplying each of these children with a personal computer with enough power to serve the kinds of educational ends described in this book [*Mindstorms*], and of upgrading, repairing, and replacing it when necessary would be about $1,000 per student, distributed over 13 years in school. Thus, "computer costs" for the class of 2000 would represent only about 5 percent of the total public expenditure on education, and this would be the case even if nothing else in the structure of educational costs changed because of the computer presence. But in fact computers in education stand a good chance of making other aspects of education cheaper. Schools might be able to reduce their cycle from 13 years to 12 years; they might be able to take advantage of the greater autonomy the computer gives students and increase the size of classes by one or two students without decreasing the personal attention each student is given. Either of these two moves would "recuperate" the computer cost. (Papert, 1980)

After several decades of research in CAI, a box score of 51 studies indicates encouraging results from CAI. "In more than 90 percent of the 25 studies (comparing) approaches, students from the CBI class received the higher scores. CBI appears to have an important positive effect on student attitudes toward computers and also appears to have a smaller positive effect on student school attitudes" (Kulik, 1983).

FIGURE 4-6 Figures 4-6 through 4-8 show children using computer-assisted instruction programs at Sesame Place. (Figures 4-6 and 4-8 are courtesy of OmniCom Associates.)

FIGURE 4-7 (Courtesy of Apple Computer, Inc.)

FIGURE 4-8

The U.S. Office of Technology Assessment has studied the potential effects of computers as instructional devices and notes that they will play an important part in the trend toward lifelong learning. Instruction will no longer be confined to the classroom. Individuals will be able to access information in their homes, their businesses, and in other environments.

> Alternative learning environments are springing up in electronic galleries like video arcades, or are the main attraction in summer computer camps. For example, "Sesame Place" near Philadelphia houses 56 microcomputers in a gallery. Users pay for computer time with tokens. "We wanted to give people free access," director Sandra Hanna explains, "but we couldn't get people off the computers." That success has led to a new Sesame Place in Dallas (Kearsley and Hunter, 1983).

As computers become more widespread, both as stand-alone devices and as a technology *within* other devices, the use of CAI will undoubtedly spread. The trend toward this growth can readily be seen: a 1980 study surveying 113 companies found 21 percent of them using CAI; in 1981, a similar survey reported that half of the Fortune 500 companies who responded were using CAI (Kearsley et al., 1981). Yet, computer-assisted instruction is beginning to look quite different from the traditional drill-and-practice or tutorial exercises.

What Makes a Computer Think It Can Teach?*

There is a simple reason why most people have such a difficult time interacting with computer-based systems. The systems are profoundly stupid. They do not learn, they cannot react based upon the effects of their actions, and they are absolutely rigid in their input/output behavior. Lately, computer systems have been called "unfriendly." This is a misnomer; mentally retarded would be appropriate.

Given this state of affairs, it should come as no real surprise to anyone that most attempts to use computers for instruction are pretty dismal. For example, consider the simplest of CAI applications: arithmetic drills. The student can type in wrong answers all day (how patient the computer is!) and often get nothing more useful in the way of feedback than "NO, TRY AGAIN." What should happen? When

*by Greg Kearsley, Ph.D.

students make mistakes consistently, the program should attempt to diagnose the problem based upon its knowledge of the kind of errors that kids make in solving arithmetic problems. An Intelligent CAI program called Buggy does exactly this.[1]

As another example consider a simulation program in which electronics technicians are learning to troubleshoot electronics circuits. A "dumb" program lets the student make various manipulations (e.g., replacing chips) and indicates whether the circuit works or not. If it doesn't work, that is, if the student hasn't done the right thing, the student must figure out why. A smart simulation program will pose questions that help students discover why their solution is wrong. The Sophie program demonstrates how this can be done.[2]

These two programs just mentioned (Buggy and Sophie) are representative of a small number of efforts in ICAI that have been undertaken in the past decade in the United States and abroad. To date, almost all ICAI work has taken place in a basic research context—as explorations of learning and teaching. However, we are quickly reaching the point where smart instructional systems could be put to practical use in real educational and training settings. For example, one current ICAI project involves the development of a smart system to teach the operation of steam propulsion plants aboard Navy ships.[3]

The major characteristics of ICAI programs are that they understand what they are teaching and what the student is learning. The idea that such programs can converse in natural language is nice but not essential. A smart system can understand what it is teaching because its subject knowledge is organized in the form of semantic networks and tutoring rules that act upon the network. This is very different from the static representation of information found in traditional "frame-oriented" CAI systems.

Smart systems are able to understand what the student is learning because they build internal representations of what the student has learned and use these to generate instruction. Traditional CAI programs keep track of how many questions or problems that a student

[1]J.S. Brown & R.R. Burton, "Diagnostic models for procedural bugs in basic mathematical skills." *Cognitive Science,* 1978, 2, 155–191.
[2]J.S. Brown, R.R. Burton, & J. deKleer, "Pedagogical, natural language and knowledge engineering techniques in SOPHIE I, II, and III." In D. Sleeman & J.S. Brown (Eds.), *Intelligent Tutoring Systems.* New York: Academic Press, 1982.
[3]M. Williams, J. Hollan & A. Stevens, "An overview of STEAMER: An advanced computer-assisted instruction system for propulsion engineering." *Behavior Research Methods & Instrumentation,* 1981, 13, 85–90.

has gotten right or wrong, but this is a very impoverished model of the student's learning progress. Thus, one of the real payoffs of smart software in instructional systems is that it can exhibit the kind of individualization we have always claimed possible but rarely achieved with traditional CAI.

So if ICAI is so good, how come it isn't all over the place? There are three major reasons. The first is that it takes pretty powerful (and expensive) hardware with lots of memory and computational power to develop and run ICAI programs. However, the currently emerging generation of 16- and 32-bit microcomputers will eliminate this problem within the next few years.

The second problem has to do with the type of software tools needed to develop ICAI programs. Traditional languages such as BASIC or Pascal are not suitable for the kind of programming required; LISP based and production system languages are needed. But the problem is not simply the existence of such tools but the scarcity of people who know how to use them. Very few individuals involved in traditional CAI have had any exposure to these languages.

Which leads us to the third and most significant problem. Smart programs take a long time to develop. Because they do not learn on their own, every single fact, rule, and inference must be programmed in. With a knowledge network of any nontrivial size, there will be thousands of links to identify. It is no accident that many ICAI programs are developed as doctoral dissertations—it literally takes years to program and debug them.

If intelligent instructional systems are to really catch on (as they eventually must), we need to do two things: develop authoring systems that make it much easier to develop ICAI programs, and figure out how to make such systems learn. I think that we will achieve both of these outcomes during this decade, resulting in a generation of computer-based instructional systems in the 1990s that will rival good human teaching. Indeed, in the future, smart software may allow us to develop instructional systems that will far exceed the ability of even the best human teachers. We should ponder the implications of children who come to accept computer systems as a primary source of knowledge and learning.

New hardware/software systems are not only becoming more "intelligent" and responsive, they are more accessible. Instead of having to find a computer and appropriate software when a need for information arises, the CAI might well be built into devices. By adding a few chips and some input-output devices, machines will be able to teach you how to run themselves. It is already estimated that almost 50 percent of all U.S. workers currently interact with a computer system in their daily jobs anyway (Kearsley, 1983).

> Embedded training consists of using the computer within a piece of equipment to deliver the training program and testing program for its operators and/or maintainers. Xerox is employing this approach for customer operator training on the Xerox 8010 professional workstation, the STAR.
>
> . . . The nature of the electronic environment should produce an acceptance of CBT seldom found in present industrial or business settings. . . . The presence of such sophisticated electronic equipment will generate a demand for CBT programs to train their users. Traditional training would be anachronistic. . . . (Hart, 1983)

Of course, using a computer or computerlike device such as a word processor or OIS terminal to do training isn't very far out of the question. We're rapidly moving from having to create and use separate instructions to deal with software like spreadsheet or mailing list programs, to having tutorials built into the software, to having software that doesn't require any teaching at all! Software systems will be able to "gauge" your level or style and respond to your increasing skills, making them usable right from the very beginning. As these systems become infused in everyday devices like microwave ovens, copiers, and so on, the distinction between CAI and "automatic" or "easy-to-use" systems will blur. Some high-ticket cars already have computer-controlled sensors for various functions, like fuel level and miles per gallon. Given accumulated data on a trip, a readout tells you approximately how many miles you've got before you need to fill up. Prototypes show computer-generated maps and displays to give you directions to almost anywhere you'd want to drive and automatically place a display of your car, heading in the right direction, on a small screen in the dash.

Just as the printed word has come to be used for so many more purposes than just formal instruction, computer-generated instruction and information will become more pervasive and used more casually. Rather than the artificially wide chasm between "video games" and drill-and-practice CAI, the new forms of electronic messages will create a new "montage" form of communication that will easily float from instruction to information to analysis to entertainment to creation to imagination—and back again.

REFERENCES

Abelson, H., *Apple Logo* (Peterborough, NH: Byte/McGraw-Hill, 1982).

Bork, A., *Learning with Computers* (Bedford, MA: Digital Press, 1981).

Burke, R., *CAI Sourcebook* (Englewood Cliffs, NJ: Prentice-Hall, 1982).

Cain, D.J., "Computer-Based Training at United Airlines," *Training and Development Journal* (August, 1981), pp. 8-9.

Clogston, T., "CBI for a High-Tech Industry," *Instructional Innovator* (September, 1980), pp. 22-24.

"Employees Learn Faster with Computer Instruction," *Training and Development Journal* (August, 1981), pp. 8-9.

Hart, F., "The Future of Computers in Industrial Training," *Journal of Instructional Development* (Winter 1983), pp. 20-26.

Hon, D., "Space Invaders, Videodiscs, and the 'Bench Connection'," *Training and Development Journal* (December, 1981), pp. 11-17.

Kearsley, G., *Computer-Based Training: A Guide to Selection and Implementation* (Reading, MA: Addison-Wesley Publishing Company, 1983).

Kearsley, G., and Hunter, B., "Electronic Education," *High Technology* (April, 1983, pp. 38-44.

Kearsley, G., Hilelsohn, M.J. and Seidel, R.J., "The Use of Microcomputers in Training: Business and Industry" Human Resources Research Organization professional paper (Alexandria, VA: March, 1981), pp. 1-81.

Kulik, J., "Synthesis of Research on Computer-Based Instruction," Educational Leadership (September, 1983) pp. 19-21.

Milner, S., and Wildberger, A.M., "How Should Computers Be Used in Learning?", *Journal of Computer Based Learning* (August, 1974) pp. 7-12.

Papert, S., *Mindstorms: Children, Computers, and Powerful Ideas* (New York: Basic Books, Inc., 1980).

Quy, N.D., and Covington, J., "The Microcomputer in Industry Training," *T.H.E. Journal* (March, 1982), pp. 65-68.

Schramm, W., *Big Media, Little Media,* (Beverly Hills, CA: Sage Publications, Inc., 1977).

Williams, D.V., and Gayeski, D., "How 'Authoring' Programs Help You Create Interactive CAI," *Training* (August, 1981), pp. 32-35.

Wolman, R., "Training with Computers," *Training News* (November, 1982), pp. 6-8.

CHAPTER FIVE

INTERACTIVE VIDEO

As engaging as computer graphics and CAI can be, nothing beats the sound, motion, and color of video displayed on the TV screen. However, traditional video programs don't provide for interaction between the program and the viewer, nor can they tailor themselves to different audiences. How do you know if people have *really* watched your advertisement or instruction?

Interactive video is the merging of the computer with video playback devices—videotape or videodisc. Started in the 1970s for military training projects, the technology quickly spread to other instructional and informational applications in business and education. Simply put, interactive video is a cross between computer-assisted instruction and traditional "linear" video. Viewers (or participants) watch a segment of video and are then asked for a response. Based on that response, they are presented with appropriate video and/or computer-generated information. It's like "talking back to your TV set." What has made this technology possible is inexpensive microprocessors and video devices that "know where they are" in playing back a program and that are capable of being remotely controlled. Both videodisc and videotape hardware can currently support interactive video, as can a wide range of micro-, mini-, and mainframe computers.

Interactive video has become the buzzword among marketing and training departments in organizations, and among educators. It is the first really new technology that individual firms can "get into" since the 1960s brought us early CAI and computer graphics, and it is being hailed as the most effective way to present information since humans learned to talk to each other. However, like other new technologies, the medium has yet to be fully developed, and many projects are still experimental. The technology "works"—mechanically, at least—but will it have the impact that its supporters predict? Studies have shown that the medium can indeed be much more effective than traditional media or "stand-up" teaching, but to produce programs that are clearly superior to other vehicles takes a wide range of both computer and video skills. The rapid proliferation of interactive video hardware and software systems and the competing claims of manufacturers have led to confusion among users and potential users. Because interactivity is something that happens between a person and a program, many programs that use sophisticated computer hardware aren't really interactive; debates go on as to just how to harness the "power" of this new technology. So, just what is interactive video, and where does it fit into the interactive communications picture?

One of the major sources of confusion about technology comes from trying to define it in terms of hardware rather than the effect or end result. Hardware provides the technical support for interactive video, but it is by no means necessary or sufficient. A more helpful perspective is to look at the other side of the technology, to the program itself, the participant, and the psychological and physical interaction between the person and the program. In this light, it's easy to see that the hardware doesn't make the interaction, the program designer does!

LEVELS OF INTERACTIVITY

Interactive video is a concept and an instructional style more appropriately defined by the outcomes of the technology for the student and instructor (Gayeski and Williams, 1980). A model of "Levels of Interactivity" developed by OmniCom Associates interrelates hardware, program design, and the information

FIGURE 5-1 Levels of interactivity (courtesy of OmniCom Associates).

	Program Design	Hardware	Questions	Response Data	Authoring
"Intelligent" System	recursive		natural language comprehended	responses modify program	specialized language/ programming
Response Peripheral	branching	specialized	motor responses evaluated	responses recorded & summarized	specialized tools/ programming
Micro-computer			constructed answers evaluated		system/ language
Responding Device				choice & latency recorded	device
Random Access			multiple-choice with feedback	via	read/write controller
Pause	linear	traditional	self-evaluation	workbook or observation	via
Direct Address			rhetorical		script design

LEVELS of INTERACTIVITY

provided to the learner and the managing instructor (see Figure 5-1). The first level is direct address. Rather than specialized technology, the technologically simple but instructionally powerful technique of scripting that "speaks" directly to the viewer is employed. This can involve asking questions for the viewers to answer "in their heads" or pointing out significant aspects of the scene. Direct address also requires a thorough understanding of audience characteristics so that the program relates its content to their styles (Gayeski, 1983). The second level, pause, structures a program with points where students are instructed to stop the program to engage in some other activity. This might be answering questions in a workbook, engaging in thought or discussion, examining an object or practicing a skill. Information for self-assessment of the activity is presented when the program is resumed.

Specialized hardware is introduced in level three in the form of a random-access controller. This simple calculatorlike device permits the playing of previously defined video segments in an arbitrary order by entering a two-digit number. This number appears within the program as the label of a section that can be selected or a multiple-choice alternative. Thus, the video "branches" to different segments depending upon the choice, providing only the information required by a particular viewer in light of his or her demonstrated understanding or expressed preference. This technology was first introduced around 1979—but not for interactive video per se. These small

FIGURE 5-2 User manipulates controls of a videodisc player to freeze frame, scan, speed up, or slow down playback of a program (courtesy of OmniCom Associates).

control pads were sold as sophisticated tape-cuing devices for locating the beginnings of different programs on one tape. For instance, sales personnel could find short segments on products related to a particular customer's application without having to fast-forward and rewind manually until the proper location was found. However, this accessibility of segments is the basis for interactive branching programs where students get feedback about the choices they make. Since these devices both record cues on the tape, and play back cues for the end user, they are an attractive way to introduce the technology in an organization. A few manufacturers, like Sony and Panasonic, make models that interface with their own "¾ or ½" format videotape players, and the controllers cost under $400.

Level four interactivity employs a responding device. This special-purpose microprocessor enables the selection of a response to a multiple choice-type question by entering one or more digits via a response panel. At this level, each response and its latency are retained by the system and summarized in a printout at the end of a session. This ability to print out responses makes these systems more attractive for many training and marketing purposes than the level three random-access units, which cannot store responses. However, level four devices are more expensive, and most have separate equipment for encoding cues and playing them back for end users; therefore, complete systems usually run for a few thousand dollars. These systems, like level three systems, store the digital information about where the segments are on one channel of the audio track, rather than on a separate floppy disk. Some responding systems also generate text screens, encoded on one audio channel of the tape, to supplement the video.

The use of a microcomputer (such as an Apple or an IBM PC) together with an interface card or "black box" linking device permitting computer control of the video device's functions, constitutes level five. Most people think of interactive video as this level—either using a videotape or videodisc playback device. This level is perhaps the most common and may become increasingly so, since many people already have microcomputers and the proper video device. In these systems, typed-in answers can be evaluated by judging models within the software, and the full range of computer functions can be used in conjunction with video. In addition, branching can occur in relation to an ongoing assessment of the student's overall progress and/or response style. Of course, microcomputer systems tend to be more expensive than the special-purpose level three and level four devices, and they are more difficult to interconnect. Usually, parts of the systems have to be supplied by different manufacturers, although some firms supply entire systems made up of components from different manufacturers for one fee.

At level six, a greater variety of responses can be assessed through peripheral devices. In many cases, motor skills can be quantitatively analyzed in the same form in which they will be performed. The skill is sensed by a specially wired version of the controls for a particular device, analyzed by the computer and then responded to by the program. A common response peripheral is a touch screen, where a user can merely point to the appropriate area of a screen to respond. Other response peripherals are bar-code readers and light pens; more sophisticated systems fall under the category of "simulators" (see the next chapter). Of course, level six systems introduce more hardware to deal with and to purchase, but they often do appear more easy to operate for keyboard novices and can evaluate skills that are closer to those required by actual jobs.

APPLICATIONS

Even though interactive video has only been around for a short time, a number of impressive programs have been produced covering a wide variety of applications. Before about 1981, most of the systems developed used specially developed hardware and software and were and are incompatible with systems on the market today. Most used the larger minicomputers rather than the micros currently popular, and some used custom-modified videotape recorders or the now uncommon optical transmissive videodisc format. Today, there are certainly a number of interactive video hardware systems on the market; although most are incompatible, at least they can be purchased off-the-shelf and comprise conventional VTRs or videodisc players. For this reason, most of the applications thus far have been for in-house use and are not being marketed to the general public. New applications are springing up every day. Once thought of strictly as a "training device," the technology is now finding its way into research, marketing, testing, consumer information, and data retrieval applications.

Interactive video has been applied in a number of industries, but perhaps the largest use of interactive videodisc is found in the American automobile industry. In 1979, General Motors purchased over 8,000 disc players for their dealerships. Software produced for this project is primarily used for point-of-purchase demonstrations by which customers can see models, features, and specifications of cars according to their reported needs and interests. Other discs in the series are used for dealership personnel and include training programs in basic selling skills, new product information, and automobile repair and service (Kearsley, 1981). The Ford Motor Company has also undertaken a similar disc project using videodisc players, as has American Motors Corporation (*Videodisc News,* 1982). At present, some 4,000 Ford dealers have interactive programs in use for sales and service technician training, motivational programs, and customer presentations. In a recent Ford survey regarding their 20-plus hours of videodisc programming (an investment of several million dollars), 70 percent of the dealers said it improved the quality of customer presentations, and 90 percent said it improved the overall quality of sales training (Broderick, 1982).

The use of this technology for sales presentations, marketing, and consumer information has been growing. Sears, Roebuck and Co. experimented with putting the Summer 1981 sales catalog on videodisc. The program consisted of about 5,600 still frames and about 19 motion sequences. Customers were able to use indexes to find the kind of product they were interested in and, from the results of the field testing, seemed to have no trouble doing so. Replication and distribution of videodisc programs can be much more economical then the bulky catalogs, and the company sees electronic communication for marketing as an important factor in its future (E-ITV, 1982). Mothercare, a maternity and children's goods chain in the United Kingdom, has installed disc players in each store to demonstrate products not easily shown on the sales floor. Research has indicated that the cost of hardware and software production has been more than offset by the quality of information provided to the customer and the freeing of sales clerks from routine or lengthy explanations.

Probably the largest number of interactive video programs fall into the category of in-house training. Corporations who had been using linear video and/or CAI have been experimenting with this new medium; however, many of its producers are companies who had never used any form of media in training. The banking industry uses interactive video technology both for in-house training and customer information. The Bank of America has produced a disc entitled "Debits, Credits, Balancing, and Stamps" for new teller training (Kearsley, 1981). The Columbia Savings and Loan of Colorado has also made a "banking" disc with one side containing basic bank selling skills for employee training and the other side containing customer information material on services, which is used in bank offices and lobbies for point-of-purchase use (Theis, 1981). OmniCom Associates has worked with Marine Midland Bank in New York to produce several tape-based interactive programs for teller training. Marine Midland had never produced either video or CAI before, but they decided that interactive video could be the answer to many of their training needs. Their first production, entitled "Your Professional Image," allows branch personnel to match up their personal goals with suggestions as to how professional appearance and behavior might help them achieve those goals.

FIGURE 5-3 Excerpts from Marine Midland Bank interactive video script (courtesy of OmniCom Associates).

Professionalism
Marine Midland Script

A typical city street at lunch time. . . . Students, laborers, housewives. . . . professionals. But how do we know *what* these people do? If you think about it, you probably put a lot of people in categories by their appearance. So who's a professional . . . and what does it mean to look and act like one?

You're a professional here at Marine Midland Bank. In fact, to many of our customers, you *are* the bank. And that's what this interactive video program is all about—being a professional and acting the part.

As a professional, you're in charge of your goals and your image—and this program will offer you some options and provide you with the information you're interested in.

All of us have goals in life—and one big step in managing your career is just reflecting on what those goals are. Coming up is a list of goals many other bankers share. When they come up on the screen, choose the *one* that's most important to you.

(computer screen)

1. *Rising in the career ladder*
2. *Being respected by my peers*
3. *Being treated well by my customers*
4. *Looking and feeling good*

Segment 2

Setting your sights on a better job is an important goal. It's natural to want to succeed and seek new challenges. Obviously, there are a number of ways you can increase your chances of promotion—doing a good job at what you're presently doing, advancing your training—and looking the part. In this program, you'll have the chance to learn about a number of techniques that can help you look like you've already got that promotion you're looking for.

(computer text)

The next section of the program will give you some pointers on the professional image. Choose the segment you'd like to see:

1. *men's appearance*
2. *women's appearance*

Segment 3

Having your co-workers like you is an important goal. Your job in the bank is people-oriented, and you've got to get the admiration of customers *and* your colleagues. But how do you do that? Well, doing a good job and being a good friend and co-worker are crucial. But how do people decide whether you're "their kind of person?" Often it's based on how they feel you add to the professional atmosphere of the bank. In this program, you can learn about what your image indicates to your peers—and how you can add that professional touch to the way you look and act.

(computer text)

The next portion of the program will show you how to achieve professional look. But first . . . would you like to see:

1. *men's appearance*
2. *women's appearance*

Segment 4

No job is pleasant unless people treat you well. Your job at Marine Midland is a professional one . . . but do you sometimes wish your customers would recognize this? How *do* customers decide to treat a bank employee? Often, it's the way the banker looks and acts. That's what this program is all about—and we'll let you decide what parts you'd like to focus on.

(computer text)

The next portion of the program will show you how to achieve the professional look. But first would you like to see:

1. *men's appearance*
2. *women's appearance*

FIGURE 5-4 Programming cues for Marine Midland Bank's *Your Professional Image,* using a level four interactive system (courtesy of OmniCom Associates).

```
*TAPE TITLE*
  MARINE MIDLAND BANK PRESENTS:

    "YOUR PROFESSIONAL IMAGE"

  >>>>START WITH SEGMENT ONE<<<<
*MAX*
  20
```

FIGURE 5-4 *(Continued)*

```
SEG.NO.    BEG.C.        LAP.T.    MULTI.   DISPLAY      T.LIMIT
    1   00:03:50:26   00:01:19:27     1    4.CHARACTER    5:00
        ANSWER  SCORE  ACCESS TO    COUNTER
            1      -        2    00:05:18:24
            2      -        3    00:05:53:06
            3      -        4    00:06:34:21
            4      -        5    00:07:05:02
            *      -        1    00:03:50:26
        ***CHARACTER PATTERN***
            WHICH OF THESE IS MOST

            IMPORTANT TO YOU?

        RISING IN THE CAREER LADDER...1

        GETTING ALONG WITH CO-WORKERS.2

        BEING TREATED WELL BY
        CUSTOMERS......................3

        LOOKING AND FEELING LIKE A
        PROFESSIONAL...................4

        *MAX*
         20
SEG.NO.    BEG.C.        LAP.T.    MULTI.   DISPLAY      T.LIMIT
    2   00:05:18:24   00:00:27:15     1    4.CHARACTER    5:00
        ANSWER  SCORE  ACCESS TO    COUNTER
            1      -        6    00:07:34:14
            2      -        7    00:09:15:20
            *      -        2    00:05:18:24
        ***CHARACTER PATTERN***
            THE NEXT SEGMENT WILL SHOW

            YOU HOW TO ACHIEVE THE

            "PROFESSIONAL" LOOK.

            WOULD YOU LIKE TO SEE:

            MEN'S APPEARANCE.....1

            WOMEN'S APPEARANCE...2

            SELECT ANSWER AND PRESS ENTER
```

FIGURE 5-4 *(Continued)*

```
      *MAX*
       20
SEG.NO.    BEG.C.        LAP.T.     MULTI.   DISPLAY      T.LIMIT
     3  00:05:53:06   00:00:33:20     1    4.CHARACTER    5:00
        ANSWER  SCORE  ACCESS TO    COUNTER
           1      -         6   00:07:34:14
           2      -         7   00:09:15:20
           *      -         3   00:05:53:06
     ***CHARACTER PATTERN***
        THE NEXT SEGMENT WILL SHOW

        YOU HOW TO ACHIEVE THE

        "PROFESSIONAL" LOOK.

        WOULD YOU LIKE TO SEE:

        MEN'S APPEARANCE.....1

        WOMEN'S APPEARANCE...2


        SELECT ANSWER AND PRESS ENTER




      *MAX*
       20
SEG.NO.    BEG.C.        LAP.T.     MULTI.   DISPLAY      T.LIMIT
     4  00:06:34:21   00:00:23:09     1    4.CHARACTER    5:00
        ANSWER  SCORE  ACCESS TO    COUNTER
           1      -         6   00:07:34:14
           2      -         7   00:09:15:20
           *      -         4   00:06:34:21
     ***CHARACTER PATTERN***
        THE NEXT SEGMENT WILL SHOW

        YOU HOW TO ACHIEVE THE

        "PROFESSIONAL" LOOK.

        WOULD YOU LIKE TO SEE:

        MEN'S APPEARANCE.....1

        WOMEN'S APPEARANCE...2


        SELECT ANSWER AND PRESS ENTER
```

Philip Morris uses disc technology to teach operators maintenance and repair of cigarette packing equipment. The discs not only contain training sequences, but also still frames of a large number of pages of repair manuals and job aids (Kearsley, 1981). Reliance Electric, an Exxon Company based in Cleveland, is also beginning to use interactive video to train its sales engineers and cut down on the traditional six-month "schools" of stand-up training.

FIGURE 5-5 Flowcharts from Reliance Electric program on bearing maintenance (courtesy of Omni-Com Associates).

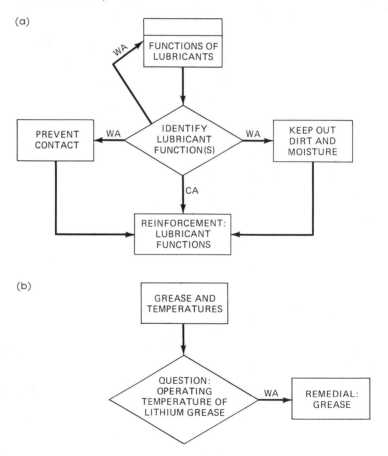

FIGURE 5-5 *(Continued)*

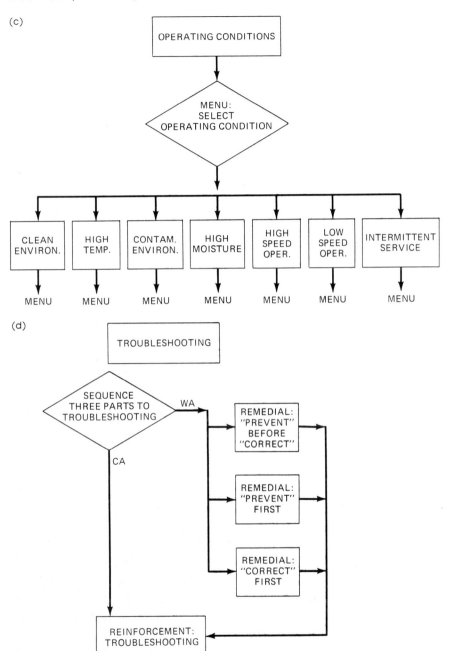

FIGURE 5-5 *(Continued)*

(e)

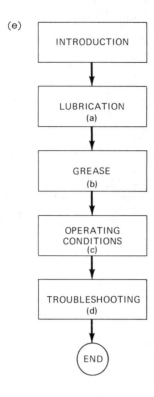

Perhaps the most sophisticated and diverse uses of interactive technologies are found in the military. The U.S. Army produced a disc, "Call for Fire," packaging a number of existing training materials such as manuals, videotapes, films, and tests, used to teach forward observer skills. A system called SIDE (soldier information delivery equipment) uses disc to store tank repair information; soldiers can use a small monitor attached to a remote videodisc/microcomputer station and thus have access to large amounts of information while actually inside a tank turret.

The U.S. Army Signal Center has a course in satellite ground station repair at Fort Gordon. The disc program used allows students to simulate manipulation of satellite station controls, thus reducing the need for actual equipment. A two-screen videodisc system is used for leadership training at Fort Benning. Trainees are presented with a potential conflict situation involving an officer and a subordinate. The trainees can choose their responses to the situation using a light pen to select options presented on the screen. The disc can present either the consequence of this decision (the experiential mode) or feedback about the appropriateness of the decision (pedagogical mode). The JOINS project allows local recruiters to show potential recruits the various military occupational specialties available and the training and duties associated with each job.

Visitors to the U.S. Pavilion at the 1982 World's Fair interacted with three videodisc programs on the theme of energy. One system featured an "energy debate" in which visitors could choose who (among several popular figures) they would like to respond to the statement on energy currently displayed. Another program provided an overview of energy sources. Viewers touched the screen to stop the program and then received more detailed information about a particular aspect. Finally, the third program featured an energy dictionary; viewers scanned through a list of words, stopped on a single word by pressing the screen, and then were presented with a definition of that term in moving and/or still color images with sound. It is estimated that 88,000 fingers interacted with the touch screens daily (Gach, 1982).

National museums and government agencies are also using disc systems for exhibits. Among these users are the Smithsonian Institution, the U.S. Post Office, the Gerald Ford Museum, and the Mexican Government Tourist Bureau (*Videodisc News*, 1982).

Some people worry that interactive video's orientation to individualized presentations will eliminate desirable group interactions. However, a form of this technology actually facilitates group discussions and participation. Mead Johnson's Pharmaceutical Division used interactive videotape controlled by a multi-user keypad system when it introduced a new drug to its sales force. The instructors were able to present information

FIGURE 5-6 Master flowchart for a St. Louis tourism program (courtesy of Interactive Image Technologies, Inc., Toronto, Canada).

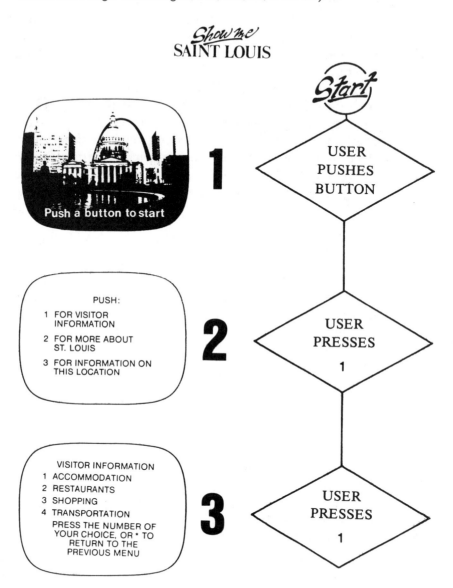

FIGURE 5-6 *(Continued)*

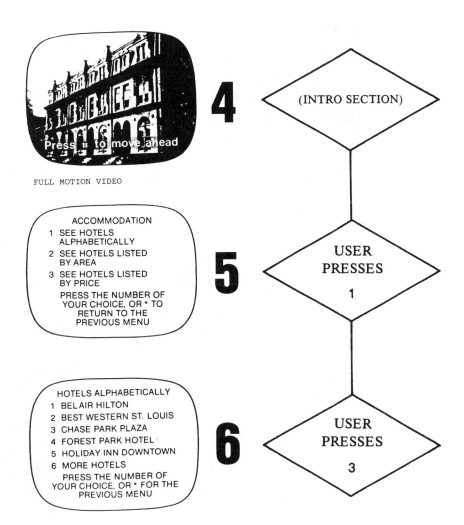

Show me
SAINT LOUIS

4   (INTRO SECTION)

FULL MOTION VIDEO

Press # to move ahead

ACCOMMODATION
1 SEE HOTELS
   ALPHABETICALLY
2 SEE HOTELS LISTED
   BY AREA
3 SEE HOTELS LISTED
   BY PRICE
   PRESS THE NUMBER OF
   YOUR CHOICE, OR * TO
   RETURN TO THE
   PREVIOUS MENU

5   USER
       PRESSES
       1

HOTELS ALPHABETICALLY
1 BEL AIR HILTON
2 BEST WESTERN ST. LOUIS
3 CHASE PARK PLAZA
4 FOREST PARK HOTEL
5 HOLIDAY INN DOWNTOWN
6 MORE HOTELS
   PRESS THE NUMBER OF
   YOUR CHOICE, OR * FOR THE
   PREVIOUS MENU

6   USER
       PRESSES
       3

FIGURE 5-6 *(Continued)*

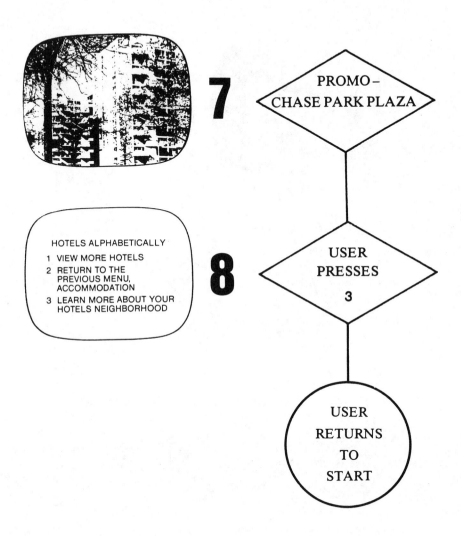

on the new product and question the sales reps. Using the GenTech MultiTerm system, sales reps were able to answer questions, and the results were then graphically displayed on the screen. The final exam was administered in this way, and the system kept track of individual scores as well as class averages (*E-ITV,* 1982).

Because of its ability to vividly simulate real life, the medical profession has been a wide adopter of interactive technology. The Robert Packer Hospital in Sayre, PA has produced a patient information interactive videotape program on chronic lung disease using a random-access controller and a ¾″ VTR. This program is used to educate patients in self-treatment procedures and motivate them to comply with recommended practices. An evaluation of the program shows that patients were able to learn rather complex information about physiology and medical treatments at a 90 percent mastery level, and that patients responded favorably to this method of instruction. Several large medical schools and pharmaceutical manufacturers have developed simulations on diseases for preservice and in-service training of physicians and nurses.

Although to date the military, business, industry, and medicine have used interactive video most extensively, the technology has found its way into higher education. The Nebraska Videodisc Design/Production Group (of the Nebraska ETV Network at the University of Nebraska, Lincoln) was created in 1978 to explore the potential of videodisc technology and to become a service agency for videodisc production. Since that time, it has been involved in the making of over 40 videodiscs, mostly for industrial clients. They also sponsor videodisc symposia and workshops on disc mastering and production (Nugent and Christie, 1982). However, they have produced a college-level interactive videodisc, "The Puzzle of the Tacoma Narrows Bridge collapse," which teaches physics principles. Using historical footage of the disaster, the system allows students to perform nine experiments, each of which can be experienced at three levels of difficulty depending upon the mathematics required and the physical principles discussed (Kearsley, 1981). This disc is now being marketed by John Wiley and Sons, Inc. (*E-ITV,* 1982). The Group has also produced a series of videodiscs in cooperation with Nebraska's College of Dentistry, which will interface still and motion sequences relating to three dental case studies with a computer-assisted instruction program (Nebraska Videodisc Design/Production Group, 1981) and a program on evidence objections for law students (Levin, 1983).

The National Science Foundation has sponsored several college-level interactive programs. WICAT, Inc. (a Utah-based computer and interactive video production company) produced a videodisc for introductory biology based on excerpts of existing films with enhancements of still frames and computer text. The disc consists of 10 lessons, reportedly about one-third of an introductory college biology course. A joint project by Utah State University and the University of Utah resulted in a program on quantum mechanics, electronics, and gravitational fields. The original was developed on interactive videotape and then transferred to disc (Kearsley, 1981). Kansas State University Department of Physics has established a Physics Activities Center, an eight-station computer-videodisc learning center. One disc is being prepared that will allow students to freeze-frame and time-video events to take measurements and analyze data (Zollman, 1982). At Ithaca College in upstate New York, a student-produced project teaches the proper form for creating behavioral objectives; another is a "point of information" program for prospective students and their parents. Each of these programs was executed using moderate-cost video production equipment and random-access, half-inch videocassette players.

On the elementary school scene, ABC and the National Education Association are collaborating on a disc project called the Schooldisc. The goal of the project is to produce 20 discs containing segments on language skills, social studies, and the arts, as well as one segment per disc on teacher training (Kearsley, 1981). A few universities have also produced materials for secondary and elementary education. The University of Nebraska Videodisc Group produced an early disc on tumbling and discs for the hearing-impaired, including captioned stories, finger spelling lessons, and simulations designed to aid reasoning processes. The Exceptional Child Center at Utah State University has also created a videodisc for the developmentally disabled using a touch screen to teach students to distinguish sizes, colors, and shapes of objects (Kearsley, 1981).

Pioneering in Interactive Video*

During the month of December, 1978, we purchased an Apple II computer, brought it home, and plugged it in. Our initial enthusiasm was abruptly curtailed when all we saw was "garbage" all over the

*by Robert and Myra Oberman.

television screen, and nothing we could do would convince our new device to perform. We learned the next day after returning to the computer store in a semiblizzard that the problem was nothing more than some loose computer chips which needed to be seated more firmly, a process we find useful every now and then without thinking twice about it. (When you do this, be sure to turn off the computer first.) We have learned a great deal since the day we purchased our computer, revision board #1, with 16K of memory and only a cassette recorder for storage. We progressed through the stages of fascination with early games. There was little if any commercial software on the market in those days. We progressed beyond the game stage, acquired a disk drive out of sheer frustration with cassette loading problems, and upgraded our 16K computer to 48K and later to 64K with a language card addition to enable us to use FORTRAN, Pascal, and now, SuperPILOT.

As an attorney and legal secretary husband-and-wife combination, we had no previous experience with computers except for dedicated word processing equipment in our law office. When we became the chairpersons of our synagogue afternoon Hebrew school a few years ago, we began to envision the possibilities of using a microcomputer in the synagogue school. We applied to a local Jewish foundation in Omaha, Nebraska, which had recently been formed for the purposes of providing initial funding for innovative projects serving the needs of Jewish youth. We received the first of several grants to implement a program of computer-assisted instruction in Jewish education. We were able to encourage our synagogue to purchase an Apple II computer for our Hebrew school. With the initial grant, we were able to obtain some general educational software for the school. However, little if any software was available for Jewish and Hebrew education and therefore we had to create these programs ourselves. Under the name of Alef-Byte Computer Software, we produced several CAI lessons in English regarding the weekly Torah readings in the synagogue, a study and quiz lesson involving the translation of the Ten Commandments from Hebrew to English, and we are now developing an authoring tool to allow Hebrew to be input directly from the video screen using a light pen. Programs using Apple Pilot include subjects such as Hanukkah and the Passover Seder. Our son, Stuart, age 12, is very proficient at deciphering documentation and has from the beginning served as our "technical adviser" in our programming endeavors.

We first observed interactive video at a local educational service unit where the consultant had created a prototype program using an Apple computer, Panasonic ½" video recorder, and a Whitney interface board and a videotape version of an Encyclopedia Britannica unit about weather. We were overwhelmed with the new educational possibilities that could result when computers were combined with video. We began investigating equipment and interface cards. We had read an article, and after some more research, purchased a BCD interface board to use with the Apple computer and an industrial video recorder.

We began by taking some prerecorded material, the first 20-minute videotape footage of "The Rise and Fall of the Third Reich," and making an interactive lesson about Hitler's early years. This seemed suited to a unit of study about the Holocaust, which is part of our school curriculum. We then became aware of the Aspen Project developed at MIT, which is an interactive travel experience which takes the viewer to Aspen, Colorado. This concept prompted us to envision interactive learning opportunities for our students to take a simulated trip to Israel and Jerusalem. Of course we do not have videodisc or television studio capabilities at our disposal as did MIT, but using existing prerecorded travel footage of places in Israel allowed us to set up an interactive videotape travelogue of several sites in Israel, which extends student experience beyond textbooks. Resources such as "Hello Jerusalem," a weekly program seen over our cable network, were used to obtain video sequences.

It was time for us to try a video production of our own. We enlisted the participation of a friend who is a local rabbi to be the subject of the lesson. Along with Rabbi Allan Gonsher, we were assisted by Peggy Saks, who is a biomedical photographer at a local medical center, and our son Stuart served as our technical assistant. We quickly had to learn about concepts such as story boards, and we found that writing a script for interactive video is not at all like writing a linear script. It was a challenge to plan multiple branching and consider all the possible reinforcement responses required by even one multiple-choice question.

We found it helpful to select a topic which would focus on a specific procedure as our initial interactive video project. All Jewish males over the age of 13 are obligated to put on phylacteries, also called tefillin, and therefore the boys require instruction about this procedure. We selected a text which explains the procedure of putting on tefillin as a guide for writing our script. We used our synagogue chapel as the setting, and equipment consisted of portable lights, our home RCA color television camera, an inexpensive lapel microphone, and a Sony ½" industrial video recorder. We had no editing equipment or sound mixers, and added musical background at the time of taping by means of an audio cassette recorder containing prerecorded music, which we turned on as needed during the taping.

The logging of the scenes using "Logger II" (part of "The Instructor" authoring system by BCD Associates) served as an editor of sorts. A menu was created at the beginning of the program providing for the student to view either the entire lesson interactively or to view individual segments of the procedure. We especially enjoyed creating a sequence dealing with decision-making, where the student is asked to make certain judgments based on material viewed in the lesson. The tool of interactive video is especially suited for presenting simulated situations calling for judgments to be made by the student. In this example, we showed incorrect behavior regarding attitudes while putting on tefillin, and a reinforcement video sequence was designed for each incorrect multiple-choice response.

One of the features we utilized was a display of computer-generated Hebrew graphics showing the appropriate Hebrew prayer which accompanies the procedure of putting on Tefillin. The audio portion from the videotape reciting the appropriate Hebrew phrases is used with the graphic so that the student can learn the correct Hebrew from both visual and audio sources.

Future projects include interactive video lessons using the newly released SuperPILOT, which is an advanced version of Apple PILOT which can be used for interactive video lessons. We are experimenting with an Omniscan interface card from Anthro-Digital which enables the Apple to use a Pioneer VP-1000 laser videodisc player. This is the same configuration used by the Minnesota Educational Computer Consortium (MECC) for a high-school economics course they are developing. For fun, Stuart has created an interactive video game using the Apple computer, BCD interface hardware, and Sony VCR, using video footage from the movie *Star Wars*, which also serves as an interesting demonstration model to show the concept of interactive video.

We have made presentations in various parts of the United States showing our work in Jewish education using computer-assisted instruction and computer-assisted television instruction. We encourage educators who are just beginning to explore the uses of computers to begin with simple CAI programs and modify them to accommodate their curricula. Computer users' groups and telephone calls to support individuals are of invaluable assistance. We also suggest to teachers to identify students who are interested and knowledgeable in using microcomputers to assist in creating computer-based educational materials.

Perhaps one of the most engaging examples of interactive videodisc is the commercially available entertainment and education program, The First National Kidisc. The program features a number of segments teaching popular children's pastimes, such as knot-tying, magic tricks, speaking pig Latin, recognizing foreign flags and pictures of dinousars, and so on. Using the pause, step-frame, scan, slow motion, and dual audio track features of laser disc players, the disc provides hours of fun and instruction.

A few interactive disc programs have also been released for the adult consumer. The Mystery Disc, produced by Vidmax, weaves together 16 different mystery stories, allowing two to six players to play detective and try to solve a murder. How to Watch Pro Football and several other related disc releases use existing pro football footage combined with analyses and commentary from coaches to improve one's skills in understanding the popular sport. Go for the Green is a demonstration disc produced for the Ford Motor Company to introduce the features of their disc communications system in dealers' showrooms. This program allows the viewer to select different holes, choose clubs, and vicariously play at several famous golf courses throughout the world.

Interactive videodiscs may become the ultimate video game medium:

> To arcade "vidiots" tired of the fuzzy-edged, predetermined computer renderings of a simian dodging barrels down the facade of a Legolike building, the arrival of the interactive laser disc is a welcome new challenge: a long-lasting, palpably real world that the viewer can actively enter. To arcade operators, laser-disc games are an elixir. . . . *Dragon's Lair* follows the dictum of the video-game industry: Make it easy to learn and hard to master. Failing that, at least make it expensive. At 50 cents a pop, the average kid will spend about $50 learning about the Lair. (Eckels, 1983).

WHAT MAKES INTERACTIVE VIDEO EFFECTIVE?

Even before the advent of interactive video, which made presentation of such branching programs much more elegant, researchers experimented with inserting questions into linear films to encourage student participation. It was found that in many of these studies, simple media and active students produced the best learning results (Schramm, 1977). Effective interactive programs rely on the synergistic combination of both equipment and design.

So, then, what is interactive video—good interactive video, that is? It can be summed up by two words: identification and attention. A good interactive program is one in which the participant can "see" himself or herself and really feel comfortable about interacting with that person on the screen. It's also a program that really holds and maintains viewer interest through posing options or questions that are pertinent and appropriately paced. Whether you need a $350 random-access controller or a $50,000 custom-designed response peripheral to accomplish this depends upon the application. But good interactive video doesn't have to be expensive, and the more affordable systems are not just for the smaller, less affluent organizations. Programs have been designed and produced using some of the lowest levels of technology (but some of the highest levels of design strategies) for companies with million-dollar training budgets.

Interactive video, properly understood and implemented, could well become a highly effective adjunct to traditional classroom teaching and established mediated self-instruction, as well as an important research tool. Using this new family of technologies, programs can be produced that:

- simulate mechanical, organic, or interpersonal processes allowing students access to additional practice in situations that would be impractical for them to encounter in actuality;
- provide drill-and-practice and tutorial instruction incorporating audio, still and moving visuals, and computer-generated text and graphics;
- tailor themselves to a variety of levels of knowledge, skill, or interest, branching to remedial or more advanced material or different examples depending upon a student's input;
- incorporate existing film, video, slide, graphic, computer, and/or text

materials into one package, which by its design mandates active student attention and participation;

- provide feedback to both the student and the managing instructor in terms of individual answers and overall progress;

- open new avenues for behavioral research and psychological assessment through the introduction of less obtrusive measures, more vivid nonverbal stimuli, and adaptive, individualized testing.

HOW IS INTERACTIVE VIDEO CREATED?

Interactive video, not unlike computer-assisted instruction, is created by writing the computer portion with a programming language, an authoring language, or an authoring system. For those who don't want to even get into computers, there are specialized authoring devices (used with level four systems) that allow you to create programs with devices not unlike video editors. Instead of merely calling up computer screens or computer graphics, the controlling program calls up video segments from a videotape or disc. But it's not really the hardware and software that creates good interactive video, it's the *peopleware*.

Seven basic competencies are needed to create credible interactive video:

1. understanding the psychological bases of interactivity
2. being able to identify and select appropriate hardware/software systems
3. applying new instructional design systems
4. constructing valid and reliable questions and formulating effective feedback branches
5. employing new scripting and flowcharting techniques
6. using programming languages or systems
7. developing appropriate production and editing techniques (Gayeski, 1982).

Not only do programs have to work, but so does the interactive environment. In some situations, people would be unwilling or unable to use the best interactive video program because the surroundings did not offer sufficient screening from distraction or afford necessary privacy (Williams, 1981).

Once you have conceptualized the kind of programs you will want to produce and the setting in which it will be viewed, selection of a hardware/software system is the next step. In interactive video, hardware selection involves much more than price and compatibility comparisons. Many systems will, in effect, dictate the kinds of programs you can design. This is where the subject of authoring languages and authoring systems comes in. Authoring languages and systems are the means by which you write the text and branching "logic" to the video portion of the program: writing questions, identifying correct and incorrect responses, and telling the system where to "branch," depending upon a participant's answer. Sometimes these authoring devices are built into the hardware, such as in level three and level four; in systems using microcomputers, the authoring language or system usually comes on a floppy disc. Authoring languages are more like computer languages, with various codes and syntax that you must learn. Authoring systems, on the other hand, lead you through the programming step by step, asking you questions about what you want to do at every stage. Although the authoring systems are easier to learn, they are much slower to use when executing programs, since you must answer each of a long sequence of questions for each command (Gayeski and Williams, 1982). Ease of use and speed, however, are not the only questions, or even the primary questions, to address when selecting a programming system. You must make sure that the device or language is flexible enough to permit you to design the kind of branches, questions, and feedback you desire for your specific purposes. For instance, some systems and devices only support single branching, which means that if a student gets the answer correct, he or she goes on; if the answer is incorrect, no matter how incorrect, only a single "remedial" branch is available for presentation. In multiple branching, you as the author can designate a different branch for each different response, say, one for the correct answer, another for a really "off-the-wall" incorrect answer, and two others for answers that are partially correct. (See Figure 5-2.) Other systems automatically come back with student reinforcement evaluating the answer as correct or incorrect. The wording or even the presence of such feedback may be inappropriate for your particular topic and audience. The choice of authoring systems is particularly

FIGURE 5-7 Interactive design and development flowchart (courtesy of OmniCom Associates).

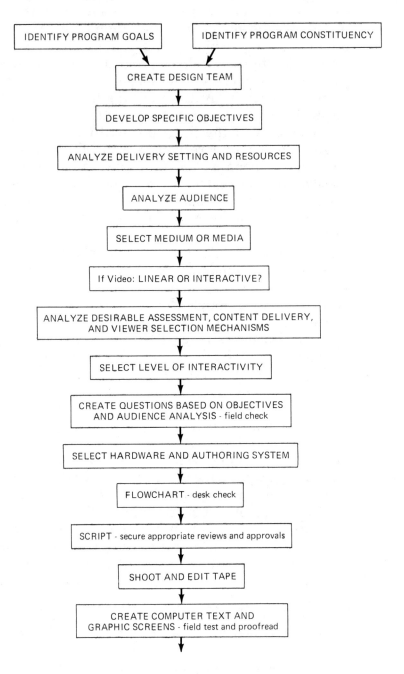

FIGURE 5-7 *(Continued)*

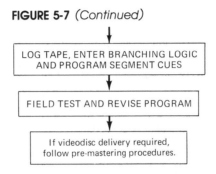

critical in starting in interactive video, because the device or program becomes, in effect, your "co-producer" (Williams and Gayeski, December, 1981).

The instructional design system used in developing your programs is also crucial. Whereas audience analysis is important for any program, in interactive video it's particularly a central issue. If you want your audience to really feel like interacting with the program, you've got to know something about their styles and needs. You've got to make that program "approachable" and "polite," not just "friendly." Second, interactive video programs are almost always the product of team work. No one can be expected to have the expertise in instructional design, video scripting and editing, question design, programming, flowcharting, and evaluation that are necessary parts of interactive production. New ways of actively incorporating the inputs of many different constituencies are needed (Gayeski, 1981; Gayeski, 1983).

Interactive video holds much potential for creative communication—whether in entertainment, sales, or instruction. As it passes out of the grips of the "high priests" of technology and becomes affordable and accessible to "ordinary people," the medium will grow even more rapidly. Unfortunately, to many people interactive video is associated with $100,000 budgets and mysterious technical skills. Once those stereotypes are broken, even more effective, truly personalized programs will be available to all of us.

REFERENCES

Backer, D., "One-of-a-Kind Video Programs," *Instructional Innovator* (February, 1982):26-27.

Bailey, H.W., "The Computer Interactive Videodisc," *Filmmakers Monthly* (November, 1980):28-11-31.

Broderick, R., "Interactive Video: Why Trainers Are Tuning In" *Training/HRD* (November, 1982), pp. 46-49.

DeChenne, J., and Evans, Robert, "Simulating Medical Emergencies," *Instructional Innovator* (January, 1982):23.

Eckels, H., "New Game in Town," *Technology Illustrated* (November, 1983), pp. 10-18.

E-ITV, "An Interactive Video Casebook," (June, 1982):35-39.

Gach, Stephen, "When Interactive Video Works," *Video Systems* (October, 1982):14-21.

Gayeski, D., "Return of the Talking Heads?", *Audiovisual Communications* (March, 1981):60-62.

Gayeski, D., "When the Audience Becomes the Producer: A Model for Participatory Media Design," *Educational Technology* (June, 1981):11-14.

Gayeski, D., "Interactive Video: Getting Into It," *Business Screen* (Oct/Nov. 1982), pp. 28-29.

Gayeski, D., *Corporate and Instructional Video* (Englewood Cliffs, NJ: Prentice-Hall, Inc., 1983).

Gayeski, D., "An Interactive Instructional Design System," *Training and Development Journal* (December, 1983).

Gayeski, D., and Williams, D.V., "Program Design for Interactive Video," *Educational and Industrial Television* (December, 1980):31-34.

Gayeski, D., and Williams, D.V., "How Authoring Programs Help You Create Interactive CAI," *Training/HRD* (August, 1982), pp. 32-34.

Gayeski, D., and Williams, D.V., "Interactive Videodisc: Is It in Your Future?", *VideoPro* (May, 1983), pp. 16-21.

Hon, D., "Respecting the Intricacies of Design," *Video User* (May, 1983).

Kearsley, G., "Videodiscs in Education and Training: The Idea Becomes Reality," *Videodisc Videotex* (Fall, 1981):208-220.

Levine, C., "Videodiscs: The Format Finally Takes Hold," *VideoPro* (October, 1983), pp. 26-30.

Meigs, J., "Going Interactive: Menu for Success in Corporate Disc Production," *Videography* (January, 1983), pp. 24-25.

Nebraska Videodisc Design/Production NEWS (Volume 2, no. 2) Fall, 1980.

Nugent, R., and Christie, K., "Using Videodisc Technology," *Video Systems* (March, 1982):16–21.

Schramm, W., *Big Media, Little Media.* (Beverly Hills: Sage Publications, Inc., 1977).

Schwartz, M., "Interactive Program Design for Corporate Training," *E-ITV* (August, 1980):35–39.

Theis, M., "Producing an Interactive Disc for Customer Use," *E-ITV* (June, 1981):32–34.

Training, "Videodisc Design: Solving Technical Headaches," (November 1983), p. 85.

Williams, D.V., and Gayeski, D.M., "The Authoring Language—Your New Co-producer in Interactive Video," *Educational and Industrial Television* (December, 1981), 50–52.

Williams, D.V., and Gayeski, D.M., "Interactive Assessment," *Instructional Innovator* (February 1983).

Williams, D.V., "An Interactive Video Module," *Videodisc News* (July, 1981).

Zollman, D., "VIP Labs," *Videodisc News* (March, 1982):5–6.

CHAPTER
SIX

SIMULATION

Now I begin a gradual descent by throttling back to about 25%. The plane drops very slowly. Willard is not in sight yet. Check the chart; Willard altitude is 754. There it is! Altitude is now 3,000, and I continue my glide. The airport is getting closer now, but I'm too high. I inch the stick forward, and I drop a little faster. 2,000 feet now, so I give 10% flaps and inch the throttle back up to 50%. Stick forward to keep the glidepath. I've got a better view of the airport now, but I'm not lined up on the runway like I had planned. I begin to adjust my course to line up. 1,500 feet, landing gear down. A little carburetor heat, just in case. . . . Hold on now. Stay on the runway, look for the taxiway. Apply some brakes. There it is. Off the runway. More brakes. Oh, heck, stomp on the brakes. The plane stops. And I stop to catch my breath. (Fastie, 1983)

Pilot training in a multimillion-dollar flight simulator? No, just Saturday afternoon at home before a flying lesson!

Considerable realism in a computer graphic display can be achieved in advanced simulators for personal computers. *Flight simulator* allows you, via an IBM PC, to pilot a small plane to any of five major areas in the United States, including about 22 airports in a variety of weather conditions. Displayed in high-resolution color graphics are the plane's controls, radar maps, and views out the plane's windshield. Major sites are complete with details of their runways and major landmarks, like the Sears Tower in Chicago. The animation moves at an incredible 15 frames per second. This system encompasses an accurate representation of the world, so you could use real aeronautical charts, if the 100-page manual doesn't have enough detail for you. Using many of the regular keys and all of the IBM's function keys, you can control everything adjustable about this simulated plane. The user can select any of 50 modes—weather conditions, aircraft reliability, and a "reality mode," which, when off, lets you fly even though you're out of gas! If flying all over North America gets too boring, you can play a game of British Ace and do combat with three Fokker biplanes!

Simulation is as much a part of our non-computer lives as the theater, games, and liturgy, ever since children pretended to go on a hunt or played with household castoffs. Many sports and games were originally maneuvers to keep soldiers in practice until the time for real battle came. However, we now have more sophisticated means for representing whole systems and events with computerization. Our human symbol-making natures lead us to create a variety of systems that model or imitate real ones to develop and practice behaviors in a setting that is free of the consequences of our imperfect skills, allowing us to experience events from a safe distance. Whether for enlightenment or enjoyment, the interactive technologies are enhancing our ability to create a realistic, responsive environment, which is the basis of any simulation.

Simulation may be used for training, assessment, or entertainment—the style may differ, but the principles remain the same: to create a situation that the participant can believe is "the real thing." In training, simulation is usually reserved for the latter stages of learning when skills developed must be combined, usually under time constraints and when various kinds of behavior-systems (such as perception, memory, and motor skills) must be integrated. As mechanical and computer systems in the real world become increasingly complex, so does the training that goes along with them. How can you teach

FIGURE 6-1 Figures 6-1 through 6-3 show a B737 simulator (courtesy of Flight Training Devices).

FIGURE 6-2

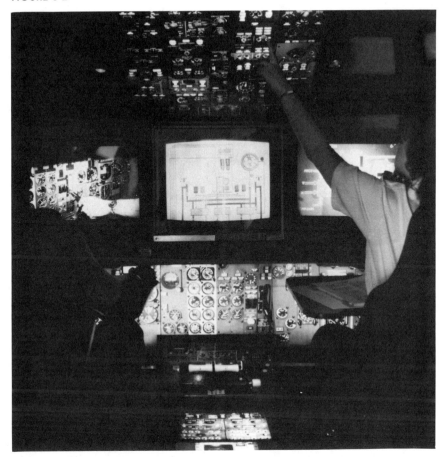

someone to safely operate a nuclear power plant . . . pilot a
submarine . . . fly a jet . . . apply cardiopulmonary resuscitation to a heart attack victim? What are the consequences when
the trainee fails? In assessment, simulation makes possible a
more externally valid test of a complex skill, as well as
providing precise feedback. In fact, one of the advantages of
interactive simulation is the combination of training and
assessment. As entertainment, simulations provide opportunities to have "safe thrills." While not an unmixed blessing, video
games have added to the outlets for competitive feelings,

FIGURE 6-3

creating a new kind of neighborhood hero, whose prowess is not based on traditional athletic abilities.

Many of us are familiar with simulators for space capsules and airplanes—devices almost as intricate and expensive as the "real" objects they simulate. The area of simulation, however, is much broader and encompasses sophisticated designs embodied in rather ordinary hardware like a small personal computer. There are two aspects of a simulation: the display, analogous to the stage set and costumes in a play; and the simulation process, similar to the script and acting. Displays in simulations are given new realism at low cost and in small size by video and graphics technology, while the imitation of processes benefits from the computers.

Some kinds of "computer simulations" are actually complete models of known processes and are used mainly to produce data to test hypotheses. While these can be used in an interactive fashion, we will focus upon simulations and simulators that model systems involving human judgment and action (such as flying a plane or making a sales call).

Technologically based interactive simulation began by

FIGURE 6-4 Diagram of a DC9 simulator (courtesy of Flight Training Devices).

II. #1. INTERACTIVE COMPUTER CONTROLLED FLIGHT GUIDANCE TRAINER

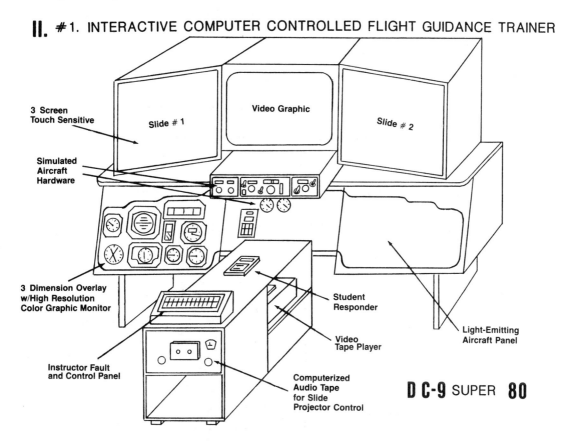

3 Screen Touch Sensitive

Slide # 1

Video Graphic

Slide # 2

Simulated Aircraft Hardware

3 Dimension Overlay w/High Resolution Color Graphic Monitor

Student Responder

Light-Emitting Aircraft Panel

Instructor Fault and Control Panel

Video Tape Player

Computerized Audio Tape for Slide Projector Control

D C-9 SUPER 80

modeling mechanical devices. Later, computer programs made it possible to model nearly any process that could be represented quantitatively. Recent video-graphic systems have added realism and introduced the possibility of simulating human interaction. Some of the most interesting simulations are those of situations requiring an orchestration of perceptual, motor cognitive, and interpersonal skills. The heart of simulation is the "display," representing the appearance of the system, and the "process," or means by which changes occur.

Everywhere, people are taking actions to accomplish change. But the processes of change have not been presented in an orderly way in our educational institutions. The dynamics of

FIGURE 6-5 Flowchart from simulator (courtesy of Flight Training Devices).

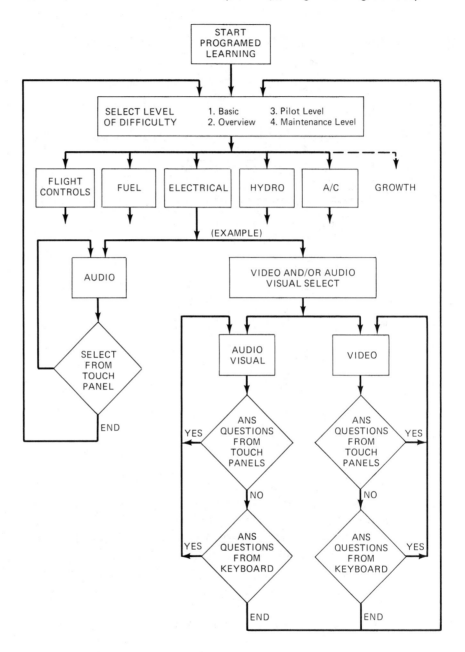

change have seldom been taught as a basic foundation that underlies all fields . . . the dynamics of changing conditions can become a universal foundation underlying all fields of endeavor. With a solid understanding of the structures that cause change, a person acquired a degree of mobility between fields. If the behavior of a particular structure is understood in one field, it can be understood in all fields. The same structures, each with its own characteristic behavior, are found in medicine, engineering, economics, psychiatry, sociology, management, and the everyday experiences of living. (Forrester, 1983)

Young Ed Link's father owned an organ factory, and it was apparent from his early childhood that he had an aptitude for science and mechanics, as he became skilled at building pianos and tuning organs. As a young man, Link became fascinated with flying, but even then, the lessons were costly; he found that he couldn't afford the necessary plane rental, lessons, and fuel. So, 24-year-old Ed began working in the basement of his father's organ factory on another kind of mechanical contraption that made his name synonymous with "simulator." The first Link trainer was built in 1929, and the next year he and his brother opened the Link Flying School. Using the simulator, they charged only a fraction of what their competition was asking for flying lessons. As the country was building up forces and skills for its entry into World War II, the simulator idea caught on, and the rest is history. From an organ factory and a young flying enthusiast was born the multimillion-dollar industry of simulators.

American Airlines Flight Academy*
Development of Simulation Systems in American Airlines

In the very early days of flying, pilots learned primarily by trial and error with relatively little guidance other than their own experience. The learning process resulted in many wrecked airplanes and, tragically, in the loss of pilots' lives. Pilot training progressed from dual-control aircraft through crude simulators (Figure 6-6) in which movement was created by attendants, through the famed Link trainer (Figure 6-7).

*by R. C. Houston, Ph.D.

FIGURE 6-6 Early flight "simulator" developed in England in approximately 1908.

FIGURE 6-7 Link trainer.

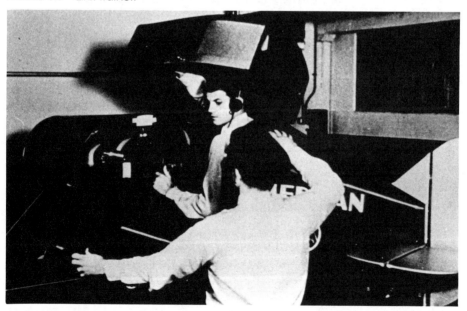

FIGURE 6-8 Interior configuration of B727 simulator.

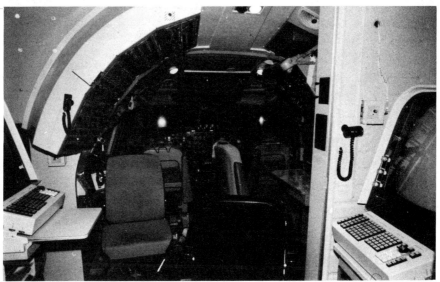

Development of Digital Simulator Systems

As the state of the art of electronic computation progressed, digital computers came into the forefront as being extremely fast processors of large amounts of complex data. I had the privilege of meeting Ed Link on several occasions, and on one tour of his factory that he personally conducted, he explained that the next breakthrough in simulation would be the capability of using digital computers. The major problem was to convert the analog outputs of aircraft instruments and control systems to digits (zeros and ones) as required for the operation of the digital simulator. Thanks to the ingenuity of the electronic and computer engineers, this problem was resolved so that it was possible to operate the simulated instruments and controls of an airplane by means of a digital computer. With this breakthrough, training devices were designed that very closely simulated or duplicated the operation of the aircraft systems and controls. Motion systems provided the basic cues for pitch, roll, and heave. A picture of one of these simulators (referred to as a three degree of motion simulator) is shown in Figure 6-8. Figure 6-9 shows the extent of the cockpit instrumentation.

As simulators progressed in fidelity, it became apparent to all concerned that there was one other major area missing from the

FIGURE 6-9 Simulator instrument panel with closed-circuit television visual scene of runway.

FIGURE 6-10 Flight simulator with three degrees of freedom motion base and television visual projection system.

simulation scene: visual cues outside the cockpit. The development of systems to meet the very high fidelity requirement for visual simulation was a long exercise that started with a simple projection of a horizon, then a runway. The development of closed circuit television made it possible to project an airport scene in front of the cockpit. Figure 6-10 shows the model board that was used for this purpose. With this level of sophistication of visual and airplane simulation, it became possible to replace a major part of airline transition training and recurrent training time with the flight simulator in lieu of the airplane itself. A study conducted by American Airlines in 1969 played a large role in demonstrating to the FAA that training regulations could be changed to permit the majority of training in the flight simulator. In 1972 American Airlines was able to demonstrate that, with the use of a three degree freedom flight simulator and a closed circuit video visual simulation system, it was possible to upgrade co-pilots to captains solely in the simulator. The next developmental step in simulation was the advent of a six degree of freedom motion base. This made it possible for the simulator to move not only in pitch, roll, and heave but also to move in yaw (from side to side), fore and aft, and rotate. Further developments in visual systems resulted in a computer-generated image that dynamically represented the airport scene. Initially, the computer-generated image was only a night display, but then it became technically possible to simulate a dusk scene and then finally a daylight scene. The latest version of a flight simulator has a six degree of freedom motion base: a digital computer that makes it possible to very precisely duplicate aircraft instrumentation and control, and a computer-generated visual system that provides an imaged focused at infinity for the forward and side cockpit windows. Such a simulator has made it possible to completely eliminate the airplane in transition and recurrent training. With the development of such a sophisticated simulator, the fourth reason for simulation has become apparent: *Flight simulation can do a better job of training the pilot than using the airplane itself.* This statement at first may seem a little hard to accept, but it is possible to do things in the flight simulator that would be unsafe to practice in the real airplane.

Introduction of
Simulation at American Airlines

The transition from airplane training to simulator training has not been easy either in the military or in airline applications. Possibly the first problem that arose was the resistance of the instructors to teaching in a "box" on the ground versus flying the real airplane. Pilots are pilots because they like to fly, and pilot instructors also like to fly. In my experience in military training and instrumentation research, I found that instructors and test pilots initially were very critical of the simulators and concentrated on the differences between the simulator and the airplane rather than emphasizing those areas where the simulator did a good job and had training value. As instructors learned to use simulators and as the simulators improved in their fidelity, they began to realize that they could do a much better job of teaching in the flight simulator, and that it also was a much safer way of teaching.

Student acceptance of flight simulators was mixed. The naive pilot didn't notice differences between the simulator and the airplane and consequently was not critical of it. When properly instructed, the pilot learned. The highly experienced pilot could recognize that there were some differences between the simulator and the airplane and tended to be critical of the simulator's performance, particularly if the pilot experienced difficulties. Acceptance of the experienced pilots was complicated by the fact that most pilots at some time in their careers had been exposed to a simulator that did a poor job of duplicating airplane performance. It might have been designed poorly or, more likely, the simulator was not maintained to the standard for which it was designed. Consequently, there was a high level of resistance of experienced pilots using flight simulators for transition and recurrent training. That resistance was overcome, however, as simulators came to represent aircraft very closely, and the pilots recognized that they could train very effectively in the device. Figure 6-11 shows a cutaway view of an up-to-date flight simulator built by Singer-Link. Figure 6-12 shows the interior configuration of the simulator, showing instructor control panels in the foreground.

Our experience at American Airlines has shown us that the syllabus of instruction must be a success-oriented syllabus. By that is meant that the syllabus is designed to maximize the probability that the trainee will successfully complete it. To do this, the trainee must first learn to operate the systems and fly the simulator under normal conditions and build up confidence so that he or she can "fly" the simulator when all systems are operating normally. Once the trainee has confidence, abnormalities may be introduced, but in a manner such that the trainee has a high probability of successfully handling them. This training approach is most important because it is possible to overwhelm even the most proficient pilot by setting up the simulation

FIGURE 6-11 Model board and television camera gantry for closed-circuit television visual simulation system.

exercises that will tax his or her capabilities to the breaking point. Unfortunately, in the initial use of simulators, instructors on many occasions used them to see what that breaking point was. This had a disastrous effect on the experienced pilot's morale and made the pilot literally hate flight simulator sessions. Not everyone can reach the necessary proficiency in a flight simulator, but its primary use is to help pilots reach their highest level of proficiency. If that highest level meets the standards set by the airline and the FAA, the pilot is successful in training. Simulators have made it possible to train to higher levels of proficiency at lower cost than using the airplane itself.

FIGURE 6-12 Cutaway view of Singer-Link Advanced Simulation Technique Simulator. (Figures 6-6 through 6-12 are courtesy of the American Airlines Flight Academy.)

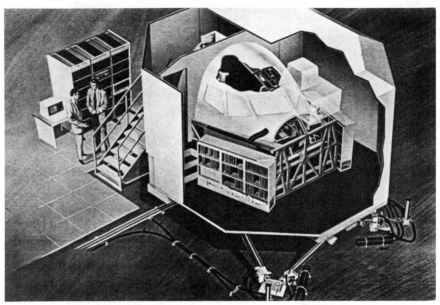

Summary

Development of flight simulation has been challenging, fascinating, and rewarding. In some ways it has seemed to be a slow and agonizing process but, on the other hand, it represents the very best in the combination of skills of training experts, experienced pilots, and electrical, electronic, and mechanical engineers. The result has been the elimination of all hazards from pilot training and greatly increased quality of the trained pilot. The world's airlines today carry millions of people with an unprecedented safety record. Flight simulation has played a major part in establishing that record.

Processes may also be simulated by quantitative models. For instance, a simulation on choosing video production houses has been developed for an Apple computer to teach media students the factors that go into estimating an editing budget. Several variables operate in this model: First, the students must choose which of two production houses to use. One has sophisticated equipment and highly trained personnel but is quite expensive. Once editing time is reserved, it must be paid for, whether used or not. If enough editing time is not reserved, it may be difficult to schedule more time to meet the deadline. Production house #2 has minimal equipment and well-trained but relatively inexperienced personnel; of course, it is cheaper, and time can be reserved freely. After selecting the production house, the students must estimate how many hours the editing job will take. The computer then multiplies the appropriate vendor's rate per hour by the estimated editing time. Finally, the users must decide how much to charge their clients: the estimated editing budget plus their fee. If they bid too high, the computer responds that the client is unwilling to pay that high a price, and the job is lost. If the client accepts the bid, the computer then responds with how much editing time was actually needed to complete the job at the selected production house. By accurately estimating the editing time needed for each of the facilities, students can see how much money they could have made if this had been a real job!

In such a simulation, many of the computer responses are generated by mathematical formulas; thus, users can go through the simulation many times making different responses and getting different results. Since the computer is so adept at simple calculations such as multiplication and division, the burden of hand calculation is eliminated, and users get much faster feedback about their decisions.

FIGURE 6-13 Example of video editing simulation (courtesy of OmniCom Associates).

```
    OK, now that you've chosen Cin-
derburg, how many hours do you think
you'll need to edit your 15-17 minute
program?

    (Remember, editing ON THE AVERAGE
takes one hour per finished minute.)

number of hours ->17
```

FIGURE 6-13 (Continued)

```
     So then, you figure tht it will cost
you 1700  dollars to edit at Cinderburg.

     Now, how much will you ask your client
to give you for the editing (including
your fee)?

     $2000



     Actually, you needed 22 hours to edit
at Cinderburg.

     Luckily, it was easy to schedule in
more hours.

     But, since you decided to charge your
client $ 2000 , you wind up with $-200
or $-9.090909  per hour for your work.
```

FIGURE 6-14 Program listing for the editing simulation (courtesy of OmniCom Associates).

```
950 SCREEN 0:CLS
960 LOCATE 4,5:PRINT"First of all, which production":PRINT"      house will you se
lect, Ace or":PRINT"    CINDERBURG? ";
970 INPUT "  -> ",W$
980 O$=W$:OO$="ace,Ace,ACE":GOSUB 60020:IF O=1 THEN 2000
990 O$=W$:OO$="Cin,cin,CIN":GOSUB 60020:IF O=1 THEN 5000
1000 LOCATE 8,5:PRINT"Please choose Ace or Cinderburg.";
1010 PRINT:PRINT:INPUT "   -> ",W$
1020 O$=W$:OO$="ace,Ace,ACE":GOSUB 60020:IF O=1 THEN 2000
1030 O$=W$:OO$="Cin,CIN,cin":GOSUB 60020:IF O=1 THEN 5000:ELSE 1000
2000 CLS:H=0:P=0
2010 LOCATE 5,5:PRINT" OK, now that you've chosen Ace,":PRINT"how many hours do
you think you'll":PRINT"need to edit your 15-17 minute program?":PRINT"
        ";
2020 PRINT:PRINT"    (Remember, editing on the average":PRINT"takes one hour pe
r finished minute...":PRINT"but it can vary GREATLY !) ";
2030 PRINT:PRINT:INPUT "number of hours ",H
2040 P=250*H
2050 LOCATE 16,6:PRINT"So then you figure that it will":PRINT"cost you";:PRINT P
```

FIGURE 6-14 *(Continued)*

```
::PRINT" dollars to edit at Ace.":PRINT:PRINT"    Now, how much money are you g
oing":PRINT"to ask your c";
2060 PRINT"lient to give you to edit":PRINT"the program (including your fee)?";
2070 PRINT:INPUT " $",B
2080 IF B>3500 THEN GOTO 10000
2090 IF H>12 THEN GOTO 2200
2100 IF H<12 THEN GOTO 2300
2110 IF H=12 THEN GOTO 2400
2200 CLS
2210 M=B-P
2220 R=M/12
2230 PRINT:PRINT
2240 O$=" Actually, you really only needed 12 hours to edit at Ace.":GOSUB 6000
0
2250 PRINT:PRINT
2260 O$=" However, since you couldn't cancel 48 hours in advance, you have to p
ay for the reserved time anyhow.":GOSUB 60000
2270 PRINT:PRINT
2280 PRINT" Since you asked your client for $";:PRINT B;:PRINT" you wind up wit
h $";:PRINT M;:PRINT" for your work, or $";:PRINT R;:PRINT"per hour."
2290 GOSUB 60041:GOTO 11000
2300 CLS
2310 M=B-3000
2320 R=M/12
2330 PRINT:PRINT
2340 PRINT" Actually, you needed 12 hours to";:PRINT"complete the editing at Ac
e."
2350 PRINT:PRINT
2360 O$=" Since time is hard to schedule, you'll have to wait until next week t
o get some more time, delaying the job.":GOSUB 60000
2370 PRINT:PRINT
2380 PRINT" You asked your client for $";:PRINT B;:PRINT" so you wind up with $
";:PRINT M;:PRINT", or $";:PRINT R;:PRINT" per hour for your work."
2390 GOSUB 60041:GOTO 11000
2400 CLS
2410 M=B-3000
2420 R=M/12
2430 PRINT:PRINT
2440 O$=" You estimated the number of hours of editing PERFECTLY !":GOSUB 60000
2450 PRINT:PRINT
2460 PRINT" Since you asked your client for $";:PRINT B;:PRINT", you wind up wi
th $";:PRINT M;:PRINT", or $";:PRINT R;:PRINT" per hour !"
```

FIGURE 6-14 *(Continued)*

```
2470 GOSUB 60041
2480 GOTO 11000
5000 CLS
5010 H=0:P=0
5020 LOCATE 3,4:PRINT"OK, now that you've chosen Cin-":PRINT"derburg, how many h
ours do you think":PRINT"you'll need to edit your 15-17 minute":PRINT"program?
          ":
5030 PRINT:PRINT:PRINT" (Remember, editing ON THE AVERAGE":PRINT"takes one hour
per finished minute.) ":
5040 PRINT:PRINT
5050 INPUT "number of hours ->",H
5060 P=H*100
5070 PRINT:PRINT
5080 PRINT" So then, you figure that it will cost you";:PRINT P;:PRINT" dollars
 to edit at Cinderburg."
5090 PRINT:PRINT
5100 O$=" Now, how much will you ask your client to give you for the editing (i
ncluding your fee)?":GOSUB 60000
5110 PRINT:PRINT:INPUT"    $",B
5120 IF B>3500 THEN GOTO 10000
5130 IF H>22 THEN GOTO 5200
5140 IF H<22 THEN GOTO 5300
5150 IF H=22 THEN GOTO 5400
5200 CLS
5210 M=B-2200
5220 R=M/22
5230 PRINT:PRINT
5240 O$=" Actually, you only needed 22 hours to edit at Cinderburg.":GOSUB 6000
0
5250 PRINT:PRINT:PRINT
5260 O$=" But, luckily, they won't charge you for the extra hours you booked.":
GOSUB 60000
5270 PRINT:PRINT:PRINT
5280 PRINT" Since you charged your client $";:PRINT B;:PRINT", you get $";:PRIN
T M;:PRINT" for your work, or $";:PRINT R;:PRINT" per hour."
5290 GOSUB 60041:GOTO 11000
5300 CLS
5310 PRINT:PRINT:PRINT
5320 M=B-2200
5330 R=M/22
5340 O$=" Actually, you needed 22 hours to edit at Cinderburg.":GOSUB 60000
5350 PRINT:PRINT:PRINT
```

FIGURE 6-14 *(Continued)*

```
5360 O$=" Luckily, it was easy to schedule in more hours.":GOSUB 60000
5370 PRINT:PRINT:PRINT
5380 PRINT" But, since you decided to charge your client $";:PRINT B;:PRINT", y
ou wind up with $";:PRINT M;:PRINT" or $";:PRINT R;:PRINT" per hour for your wor
k."
5390 GOSUB 60041:GOTO 11000
5400 CLS
5410 M=B-2200
5420 P=M/22
5430 PRINT:PRINT:PRINT:PRINT
5440 O$=" You estimated the editing time PEFECTLY !!":GOSUB 60000
5450 PRINT:PRINT:PRINT:PRINT
5460 PRINT" Since you decided to charge your client $";:PRINT B;:PRINT", you win
d up with $";:PPRINT M;:PRINT" or $";:PRINT R;:PRINT" per hour for your work."
5470 GOSUB 60041:GOTO 11000
10000 CLS
10010 LOCATE 8,6:COLOR 23,0:PRINT"S";:COLOR 23,0:PRINT"O";:COLOR 23,0:PRINT"R";:
COLOR 23,0:PRINT"R";:COLOR 23,0:PRINT"Y";:COLOR 23,0:PRINT",   ";:COLOR 23,0:PRI
NT"Y";:COLOR 23,0:PRINT"O";
10020 COLOR 23,0:PRINT"U ";:COLOR 23,0:PRINT"O";:COLOR 23,0:PRINT"V";:COLOR 23,0
:PRINT"E";:COLOR 23,0:PRINT"R";:COLOR 23,0:PRINT"B";:COLOR 23,0:PRINT"I";:COLOR
23,0:PRINT"D";
10030 PRINT" ";:COLOR 23,0:PRINT"!";:COLOR 23,0:PRINT"!";:COLOR 23,0:PRINT"!";:C
OLOR 23,0:PRINT"!";:COLOR 23,0:PRINT"!":PRINT:PRINT"
       ";
10040 COLOR 7,0:PRINT:PRINT" Your client just won't go for that":PRINT"  high
a price.":PRINT:PRINT" Why don't we just forget this hap-":PRINT"  pened and
try the simulati";
10050 PRINT"on once":PRINT"   more ? ";
```

But simulation is not defined by hardware; it is a style of presentation. It teaches or communicates by letting the user or users explore a situation defined by a model. Instead of direct teaching (telling the participants whether they are correct or incorrect, for example), a simulation lets them discover this for themselves. Instead of calling up a limited number of "branches" to responses, a simulation can calculate a myriad of responses depending upon the number and type of user inputs. Of course, this kind of presentation is difficult to conceptualize and develop.

HOW ARE SIMULATIONS DEVELOPED?

The first requirement for a simulation is that the designer develop an accurate *model* for the situation. The model does not necessarily have to be a mathematical one. For instance, a model for sales calls might be developed wherein successful and unsuccessful types of selling behaviors are identified. Once these behaviors are defined and categorized, the model developer must discover how these behaviors are to relate to each other, how often each behavior should be used, and how certain techniques interact with buyer behavior. This kind of model has been developed by many sales organizations and consultants, based upon an analysis of hundreds of sales calls. Once a model has been defined and validated (tried out to see if it really works), one might try to teach the model to a group of salespeople who were not particularly successful to see if it improved their performance. Then, a simulation might be developed around that model. For instance, a typical buyer might be presented via videodisc, and the trainee could be presented with a list of questions or comments to choose from. Depending upon the behavior category of their choice, the simulated buyer would respond in the likely fashion. Such a simulated sales call has been developed using the PLATO computer-assisted instruction system by Commercial Credit Corporation (Kearsley, 1983).

Roberts, et al. (1983) define a number of stages in model development: (1) problem definition (2) system conceptualization (3) model representation (4) model behavior (5) model evaluation (6) policy analysis and model use. Underlying this process is the *systems approach*, whereby all elements that figure into a situation are considered an integrated system. For instance, in the video production house simulation, elements of the system are the production houses, their fees, their speed of editing, their policies for charging for unused time, their availability of time, the estimated time for completing the editing, how much the client will pay for the job, and how much the student user decides to bid for the job. Once a model is conceptualized, numbers need to be attached to the variables. For instance, how much faster is the expensive production house than the cheap vendor? In the simulation excerpted here, it was judged that the expensive house could complete the job in 12 hours, whereas the inexpensive house would take 22 hours. However, it is possible to make money using either house, depending upon how accurately you bid.

APPLICATIONS OF SIMULATION

The power of interactive video to simulate conditions that are rare, dangerous, distant, or otherwise difficult for trainees or researchers to encounter is one if its most significant attractions. This is especially true in medical training situations. The Allied Health Institute of South Oklahoma City Junior College has produced a videodisc/microcomputer program to simulate medical conditions, complete with a visual and auditory data bank of video events, enacted scenes, shots from existing media, and graphic displays and sounds of medical equipment coupled with measures of patient symptoms generated by microcomputer. Students follow an assessment procedure, and in response to their requests, the system provides the appropriate data. For instance, if examination of the patient's eyes is selected as a diagnostic step, a video image of the pupil appears on the monitor. The system also reports errors and lets students experience the consequences of their choices. For instance, if the student recommends an inappropriate treatment, the video patient may respond by having convulsions (DeChenne and Evans, 1982).

Perceptronics' "MK Series Gunnery Trainers" combines microcomputer, videodisc, and electronic game technology. The system simulates gunnery practice and includes entertainment features. The Tactical Video Map (TVM) system contains a microcomputer that controls a laser videodisc and graphics generator. Upon user request, the microcomputer selects a map background from the images stored on the disc, then adds to it graphic symbols representing tactical data including vehicles, boundaries, and facilities. The map background and the tactical overlay are displayed on a standard video monitor. Using a joystick to pan and zoom, the user moves over the mapped area. As map location or scale is changed, the tactical symbols are automatically placed in the proper geographical position (Levine, 1983).

Interactive video simulations can be used for individualized instruction in a variety of content areas. For example, at Ithaca College, students have produced an interactive videotape to teach television studio lighting and portable video operation through simulation. The Career Planning Office has also produced two interactive videotape programs with the assistance of the School of Communications faculty and students. The small staff of Career Planning has difficulty in scheduling all the students who desire assistance, especially just before graduation. To reduce the repetition of basic information and yet provide a personal and convenient service to students, the Office has produced an interactive tape on job interviewing. Turning the situation around, the student-viewer takes the role of the job interviewer, selecting which questions he or she would like to ask the "candidate" by selecting from a "menu" on the screen, to which the videotaped candidate replies. By taking the role of the interviewer, students experience the information exchange from another perspective, imagine how he or she would reply if asked that question, and see how the candidate in the program handles the situation (Andrade, 1982). Another interactive videotape simulation was produced for use in peer counselor training.

Simulations can also occur as "scripts" of human interaction. Newly hired salespeople are often trained by having them simulate a sales call with a peer or trainer acting as the customer. Simulation can be supported by physical models of real objects, either actual size or scaled up or down. These two approaches, however, are limited by credibility and transferability of skills to the job, in the first case, and expense and awkwardness, in the latter. Therefore, most models or simulations are now being carried out using computers—at least as the "brains" behind driving other physical objects or media presentations. One of the first interactive videotape-microcomputer simulations was developed by the National Technical Institute for the Deaf (Rochester, New York) to assist deaf students in practicing speech reading and job interviewing skills. The student first fills out a typical job application displayed on the screen by typing on the microcomputer keyboard. Then, the videotaped interviewer appears on the screen and asks questions based upon the general information provided by the application. The student answers by typing in a response, and the interviewer responds accordingly (the microcomputer program having analyzed the student input and branched the tape to an appropriate segment). If the student is unable to understand the interviewer's question, he or she can ask him to repeat, just as in real life. After three tries, the interviewer looks a little upset and writes the question down on a piece of note paper. The ability of interactive video to simulate a stressful and challenging interpersonal situation before actually encountering it is a unique contribution to the education process.

Some simulations re-create situations involving both technical and interpersonal skills. The American Heart Association faced the problem of increasing the number of individuals trained in CPR (cardiopulmonary resucitation). The group predicted that 10,000 lives per year could be saved if the number of CPR-trained people could be raised. Traditional means of training—group workshops using a "dummy" to practice—with had reached their limit of participants. Not enough trainers could be found to offer the instruction at times and places convenient to attract more participants. The solution: the creation of a self-teaching system using a videodisc, Apple computer, two monitors, a light pen, one button, and a specially wired Resuci-Anni mannequin. Learners can approach the system individually and are coached patiently by a pleasant physician on the videodisc. When ready, the student can practice on the dummy. Delicate and accurate sensors give feedback via the computer and videodisc as to how the student rescuer is doing. Is the compression placed correctly? Is it too deep? Too fast? In addition, the system simulates a co-rescuer with whom actions must be coordinated. Assessments in progress indicate that the system is better and faster than the traditional approaches. The system is also used for recertification of CPR-trained individuals. They can receive instruction, then actually take the test right on the system to become certified again.

CPR Videodisc with Anatomical Keypad*

Some 80 million people told a Gallup Poll in 1980 that they wanted to learn Cardiopulmonary Resuscitation in the near future. Thus the resources of the American Heart Association seemed quite in need of some sort of breakthrough . . . That agency, embodied by the AMA and all other acronyms to teach this skill of arresting cardiac arrest to the general populace, had "only" taught 15 million people to perform CPR in 15 years. Perhaps that feat of instruction pyramiding was laudable— and even unsurpassed in modern education—but it did not console the 19 out of 20 heart attack victims who still had no rescuer and who might die, perhaps within earshot of an ambulance.

It seemed to a few of us that the Space Invaders, drawing people of gaming bent to the arcades, were also capable of demonstrating a kind of teaching which could solve very large problems, by concentrating the teaching in the design of the learning experience. A fixed point of leverage was necessary for 80 million to be even considered a possibility. Fortunate or not, I was National Training Manager of the Heart Association at the time and perhaps due to a background of video and technology I gained at Texas Instruments, I became Director of Advanced Technology Development and a champion of videodisc/ micro instruction a good while before I, and probably anyone else, really knew what we were talking about.

What we did know was that the system which was to accomplish both instruction and total certification in this well-defined medical procedure would have to break some ground. We would set out to fashion a mannequin with enough sensors to create a "picture" in the mind of the microcomputer, a pattern recognition system to totally replace an instructor's observation of that complex set of CPR performances.

The videodisc, on the other hand, would be the warm and visually precise method by which the system could provide instant feedback in as many ways as the student needed to perform well quickly. The two parts, then, a sensory pattern with perhaps 4,000 variables, and instant personalized video feedback to achieve coaching, were the first two parts of the system we had to work out. The videodisc part became significantly more difficult when we confronted the problem of random-access audio, a technique of integrating sound from source other than that available in the motion-video sound track, to allow—in

*by David Hon.

our case—about 12 total hours of branching to be encased on one 30-minute side. We managed that by creating a random-access audiotape system which, by running all tracks in the same direction, gave three times the normal tape access speed by "wrapping" 15-minute sections down through three of the four levels (with "C" as control track). Therefore, if a need for random-access response fell within a 15-minute command zone, we could equal the 5-second max speed parameter of the videodisc machine.

All of this concentration on one side of the disc seemed incredibly necessary to me, in order that the student has a "manageable universe" which responded rapidly to his every performance and every need with utter transparence. For the student to have to flip the videodisc and reboot the computer would not have been in the spirit of the video games and would not, we felt, make 80 million people participate very joyously.

Before I left the CPR system in the hands of the American Heart Association and its marketing agency, (to start a new company, IXION, to produce more of this kind of "videoware" for more purposes), we saw some fairly incredible results on the validation. That validation was conducted at the University of Pittsburgh School of Nursing, and basically, the goal was to show that the system could instruct as well as a live instructor. They set 50 students as a control group, taking CPR from the conventional live instructor. Then, in a close but separate place, they set up a learning center, wherein 50 students learned from the computer/videodisc system. Then students from each group would go "across the hall" to be evaluated on a first-pass, no remediation basis by a live evaluator who gave the standard performance test. We had counted on the system merely performing as well as a live instructor. But even we who had been working on the project for three years were quite surprised at the results. Three times as many people who took CPR by video/micro passed the evaluator. And although time was not a factor in the testing, this and other testing sessions show a marked time differential, with students quite usually taking only half the time to be certified on the video/micro system.

It would seem to me, in retrospect, that the outstanding results may be attributable not only to fortunate hardware accomplishments— off the shelf and custom-made—but by the general style and tone of the whole context which was created. We wanted the student to feel that this system was "open" to student choices and widely varying performance. And perhaps most importantly of all, we wanted the users of the system to feel it "cared" about each individual student in a unique

FIGURE 6-15 CPR instruction system (courtesy of Actronics, Inc.).

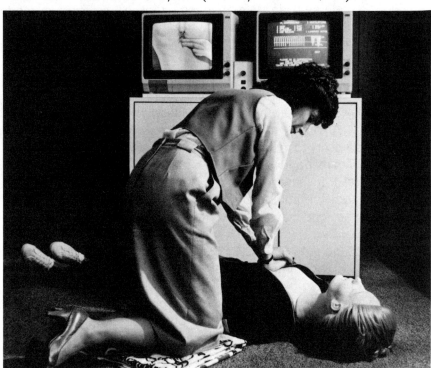

personal way. For its many efforts at this "openness" and "caring" the system has been accused of having artificial intelligence—and one would suppose that a logical extension of that would be artificial "warmth."

If there is any reason for the successful performance of this system as it goes now into the world to do its job, I would posit that it is not because of any artificial intelligence and artificial warmth. No mechanical system can do that by itself. And perhaps there is really no such thing as man-machine communication. I would prefer to think of every system, of every machine, of every product, in fact, as a human-to-human communication through an interposed medium. In that way, the "artificial intelligence" is really just the transposition of the outstanding human intelligence of our development team. As for the "artificial warmth," the sense of the system "caring" about each individual student, that is nothing in the world less than a direct transmission of our warmth and our caring—through that system. And there is nothing artificial about that, at all.

As complex as this CPR system is, the American Heart Association has gone one step further—teaching the advanced medical techniques and interpersonal skills used to keep a victim alive once he or she has reached the emergency room. The Advanced Cardiac Life Support simulation (ACLS) is also a videodisc system, this one simulating the interactions of the entire medical team called on during a cardiac crisis. The user acts as team leader, requesting tests, ordering administration of drugs, and calling for electric stimulation of the heart. The other members of the team represented on the videodisc monitors react to your instructions (if you do nothing long enough, they suggest going out for coffee!).

Vicarious travel is a unique simulation modality in which the viewer seems to turn left or right, pause to move closer to an object of interest, or even converse with a passerby. These choices are indicated by touching symbols or parts of the scene. In one version, the viewer's chair is wired to convey the desired changes in orientation. These systems usually involve two or more videodisc players, a minicomputer, a color graphics processor, video special effects hardware, and a monitor with a touch-sensitive screen.

The kind of simulation that is perhaps the most intriguing is that which takes place in a *simulator*—a specially designed physical space replicating a real environment like a plane cockpit, a nuclear reactor control room, or a ship's bridge.

As the plane taxis up to the terminal gate, from the cockpit you can see the glowing wands guiding the aircraft into position. The engines slow, the jarring vibrations cease, and there is the soft thud of the passenger boarding bridge bumping the aircraft wall. When you open the door at the rear of the cockpit, you fully expect to see a cabin full of passengers. Instead, there is a high, white room with a row of computers against one wall. It seems like Rod Serling should step up and welcome you to the Twilight Zone.

Nothing inside the cockpit of a flight simulator hints that it is a landbound contraption rocking to and fro inside a room. The instrument panel looks correct in every detail, and all the instruments function. The windows show computer-generated images of the surrounding landscape—runway, airport, lights, clouds, and sky. Mounted on hydraulic pistons, the cockpit can be pitched in any direction so fast that what feels like the buffeting of wind shear and the forces from turning, acceleration, and climbing make seat belts necessary. The sounds of flight are synthesized at realistic levels, from the whine and roar of the jet engines to the splatter of raindrops on the windshield. Sensations of flight are everywhere; the thing even smells like a plane. (Sorenson, 1983)

Simulators are also being used to teach Navy and Merchant Marine personnel to operate ships. The U.S. Navy might be the largest user of simulators—everything from nuclear power generators, submarine navigation, and radar interpretation to maneuvering ships into a harbor. Of course, all branches of the military have complex combat simulation systems.

Currently researchers are debating about exactly how much realism is necessary to make a simulator really effective. Some say that the extra millions needed to add detail are wasted, and that trainees can learn as well or better from less elaborate representations. What is essential is the overall effect that induces the same "willing suspension of disbelief" as a good play. The Maritime Institute of Technology and Graduate Studies in suburban Baltimore is using perhaps the most sophisticated and realistic ship's bridge simulator for training purposes. The ship's bridge is used to train Merchant Marine masters in the complex skills and concepts needed to safely pilot today's large commercial vessels. Two simulators, each a replica down to railings, instruments, and the winding stairs used to approach the bridge, sit in a building the size of a couple of football fields. These simulators, along with a few older and less complex ones on specific maritime control systems, are used in a variety of demanding courses needed to advance oneself through the ranks of the Merchant Marine. Although it's easy to become caught up in the glamour of the technology, Max Carpenter, one of the developers of the ship's bridge simulator, points out the importance of the participant's belief in the simulation.

"MITAGS"*

The Maritime Institute of Technology and Graduate Studies began operations in 1972 with three of the world's most advanced and sophisticated computer-based simulators. These have been constantly updated over the years. The first of the original three is a liquid cargo simulator teaching the dynamics, stress factors, and safety procedures of loading liquid cargo. The second is a steam engineering/propulsion simulator demonstrating the interaction of bridge control and steam plant operation. The third is a radar simulator with eight own ships.** Four target ships can be assigned to each of the own ships. The course and speed of target vessels can be programmed or controlled by the instructors. All of the eight own ships and their associated target ships can be assigned to the same gaming area for real-time interaction between the vessels.

Since the installation of the original simulator, several other trainers have been installed. Two of these are ship's bridge simulators evolved from a concept in use in Germany.

The MITAGS ship simulators are different in that they present many more advanced features, like 360-degree field of view, full instrumentation, motion, and realistic visual feedback. Our primary goal was to produce a nocturnal simulator using the scene as seen from a ship during the night. However, we specified the system to be compatible with a daylight scene when one that was satisfactory became available. Daylight scenes are generally computer-generated; unfortunately, this approach is tremendously expensive considering the quality of the picture. Through the years, developments have made possible a system using lasers to enable us to create daytime scenes as well as nocturnal.

The simulator right now is capable of reproducing the characteristics of any ship we wish to program. This programming process involves coming up with a complete mathematical model of every hydrodynamic aspect of a given ship, such as its turning rate, the effects of weather, the type of acceleration, deceleration, and trim and draft variables. Our trainer bridges can approximate the configuration and consoles of a wide range of ships. The equipment generates

---

**"Own ship" is used to designate a ship from one's own perspective.

*by Max Carpenter.

readouts appropriate to the situation, including radar scopes and other navigation aids, depth finders, and radio telecommunication.

As a master navigates a simulated ship, it appears to move through the open sea or through a harbor. Hundreds of situations can be set up by varying the type of ship, the weather, cargo conditions, the harbor, buoyed channels, and the type and location of other vessels in the area. The nighttime simulator shows the lights of ships and navigationally significant objects as they would really appear after dark and produces a visual scene corresponding to conditions as set up by the instructor. A motion base used with one of the simulators allows the ship to roll and pitch in the waves.

The instructors operate from a control room where the presence of other ships and weather conditions can be manipulated. Because one control room serves both simulators, the layout took a lot of careful thought by the designer so that information necessary to evaluate the students is readily available. In addition, the control room has all the instrumentation necessary to start up the simulator, change to any of the 120 programs you might want, and, of course, includes methods of designing new exercises.

As technologically advanced as the equipment is, one of the most effective aspects of the simulator is role-playing by the instructor and other students. We find that the interaction in which the instructor plays the part of the captain of another vessel or tug, chief engineer, or any one of the manned positions aboard ship, is one of the most effective aspects of this training. The instructor must make his or her communication plausible, and it is important that the instructor be assertive enough to sound genuine. In other words, if the student calls requesting information on another vessel, the instructor can respond as the captain of that vessel; by indicating what his or her intentions are—to come right, left, stop, and so forth. The student can also contact another section of his or her own vessel, and the instructor will also play that part.

In an "interactive mode," we can hook the two simulators together so the simulator "ships" can see one another. In this way, two trainees on their individual "ships" can interact through the visual scene and by voice communication. At a future date, we will add two other bridges so eventually we can have four bridges interconnected for real-time simulation. This adds another dimension of reality and stress that can't be achieved by a computer program alone. For instance, the student master of a ship can enter a harbor and see perhaps four other vessels. On a computer-only program, the student might assume that each vessel will move at a given fixed rate of speed. But with the instructor or another trainee acting as a master of the other vessel, the human variable can be incorporated into the exercise.

We were very careful to design the simulator to look as much like a ship's bridge as possible. When professionals see anything that looks phoney, from then on the whole experience begins to degenerate into a game rather than an instructional exercise. For example, when experienced masters see the simulator for the first time, their reaction is "Hey, this looks like a real ship." Most of them sense the possibility of a meaningful training experience. After a short time working with the simulator, the students usually want to try all sorts of experiments. Things that they'd always wanted to do while maneuvering, they now can try. For example, one man wanted to see if he could turn the ship in a tight area of a harbor he visited frequently. He tried it and found that it couldn't be done. His reaction was this, "I've always been tempted to try this. I'm glad I tried it here rather than with my ship!" At MITAGS, we've developed and are using the most sophisticated, realistic simulator for maritime training to date—yet it's only just the beginning.

REFERENCES

Fastie, W., "Flight of the 5150," *Creative Computing* (February 1983), pp. 77–85.

Forrester, J., "Foreword" in Roberts, N., et al., *Introduction to Computer Simulation* (Boston: Addison-Wesley, 1983).

Kearsley, G., *Computer-Based Training* (Boston: Addison-Wesley, 1983).

Roberts, N., et al., *Introduction to Computer Simulation* (Boston: Addison-Wesley, 1983).

Sorenson, P., "The Next Best Thing to Flying," *Technology Illustrated* (June, 1983), pp. 21–26.

CHAPTER
SEVEN

INTELLIGENT
SYSTEMS

"Can a machine think?"

"Sure, they can do math a lot faster than I can."

"No, I mean really think."

"Well, a CAI program can teach you things, ask questions and tell you whether you got them right."

"But you can't just walk up to one and ask it anything you'd like to know."

This conversation is a lot like many discussions about "intelligence." What do we look for before concluding that someone—or even something—is "smart"? There are usually many things that go into our definition, because meeting one or two criteria usually leads us to say, "That's not 'real' intelligence." However, no matter how many "intelligent" things an animal, person, or machine does, we may be reluctant to accord it the honor of being as smart as we are. We have gotten around this problem by calling such apparently intelligent behavior in animals "instinct"; in children and "primitive" people "cleverness"; or in the case of computers, "artificial" intelligence. When we are not really prepared for a system to be too much like ourselves, it seems like our definition of "intelligence" keeps stretching. On the other hand, once a machine can do something, we tend to take it for granted because we can understand what logically and mechanically went into the process. Once we know how the trick is performed, it isn't magic anymore, just "skill." So intelligence seems to be whatever a person like us can do but a machine or animal can't.

Several criteria probably play a role in our impression of intelligence. Of course, responsiveness to the environment is one cue. Using (our) language is important—understanding conversation, responding in a similar manner. Having information is another criterion. Does it know things? Can you ask it questions? In addition, things we would want to call intelligent can infer, go beyond the information given without "having to tell it everything." Solving problems, using an appropriate strategy for relating its information, is another characteristic. Finally, can this person or thing learn or profit by experience? Does it act differently because of previous exposure to some information, person, or method?

From general alertness to learning covers a lot of ground. If we encounter one or two of these characteristics, especially where we least expect it, the others may be taken for granted.

We may project or overgeneralize to conclude that there is more "intelligence" than there is. (Of course, the reverse is unfortunately true, too.).

Well then, using these criteria, can computers think? How do we tell whether a "system" is "intelligent"? Alan Turing, an early worker in the area now known as "artificial intelligence," offered an answer that has become known as the "Turing Test." In one room would be two identical keyboard terminals. In the next room one would be attached to a supposedly intelligent system, while at the other a person would sit. If people brought into the first room to converse via the keyboards could not tell the difference between talking to the system and talking to the "real" person, the system in the other room would be declared "intelligent." Intelligence is in the mind of the interacter.

Unlike the media we have dealt with in the previous chapters, "intelligence" is a *theme* running through all new technologies, and it is an important future trend. We have seen how computer graphics, CAI, interactive video, videotex, and simulations are all seeming to be more intelligent.

Responsiveness is seen in computer systems as search time in interactive programs and the ability of a system to make use of such things as touch screens. Even pretty commonplace devices can "do" things by themselves. Take an ordinary home thermostat, for example. It has the ability to sense its environment (a thermometer) and knows when to turn on the heat when the temperature drops too low. It continues to sense the temperature as the furnace runs, and when it reaches the desired temperature, it turns the furnace off again. Of course, this example of self-modification is routine and simple, but more sophisticated machine processes rely on similar sensing-processing-modification-sensing loops. This type of system is called *cybernetic*, a term you may have heard associated with very high-powered machines, but which is actually much more of a commonplace quality than might be expected.

Language use by intelligent systems begins in rather primitive recognition of written or spoken words and extends to "intelligent" conversation. An early conversational program, "Eliza," was written as a spoof of nondirective therapy where one's statements seem to be repeated by the therapist. (Of course, the real professional skill is being able to indicate the patient's feelings by reflecting what the patient says.) While this tongue-in-cheek therapeutic conversation may appear intelligent, the computer is actually responding to some common inputs like "you" and "because" with stock phrases. The program can also "remember" responses to make it seem like it's paying attention. Here's a variation of an Eliza-type conversational program written in Apple PILOT which we "interviewed."

FIGURE 7-1 Interaction with "Professor Media" (courtesy of OmniCom Associates).

```
The Professor is now available for your questions.

Hello.  I'm Professor Media.

What's your name?

>Diane

Always glad to see you, Diane.
So, what's your question?

>What should we tell our readers about interactive media?

I can't say.

>why not?

Why do you want to know, Diane?

>Just curious.  What would you like to talk about?

Me?

>Who else.  Yes you, Prof. Media

Can you state that as a behavioral objective?

>Ok, you're an educational technologist, then?

I don't discuss personal issues; let's talk about media!

>Ok.  How can we create good interactive media?

With great difficulty.

>I see.  How do we start?

Easy, Diane, if you know how!

>What's the first step?

Nothing.
```

FIGURE 7-1 *(Continued)*

>And after that?

Could we please change the subject?

>Why?

You'll have to call in an instructional designer on that one.

>Are you afraid of giving away your secrets?

Let's get back to your media questions.

>Why is interactive media so neat?

Well, it's logical, isn't it?

>I guess so. People like to talk to machines like you!

That's your opinion, Diane, not mine!

>Do you like to talk to machines?

They don't let me talk about myself - please ask me a question about media or I don't get paid!

>Who's they?

C-3P0.

>He's a movie star, isn't he?

And you call yourself a media person?

>Well, I thought so until I met you.

Where did you learn your communication skills?

>Ithaca College. Where did you study?

I'm not supposed to talk about myself.

>Ok. Where's a good place to study media?

Ithaca, New York.

>Thanks. Anywhere else?

Where do you think?

>I'm not too sure. What shall we tell our readers next?

Let's change the subject, Diane.

>Yes. How much does interactive media cost?

Several.

FIGURE 7-1 *(Continued)*

>Several dollars?

If the program is produced well.

>I heard that some interactive programs cost millions; is that true?

No.

>How did you find that out?

Let's talk about YOU, not me!

>You seem to be a bit shy!?!

>I see you're not talking about yourself.

That's too bad, Diane, but I can't do anything about it.

>Who programmed you?

Let's talk about YOU, not me!

>Well, I wasn't programmed. Where do you live?

Do you mean ME?

>sure you, Prof. Media...

So what is it you want me to tell you?

>where do you hang out?

Me?

>yes you, stupid!

Can you state that as a behavioral objective?

>Back to that again. Are behavioral objectives that important?

Yes.

>why?

Because I said so, Diane!

>why do you think so?

Little ol'me?

>yes.   Why are behavioral objectives important?

For no reason whatsoever.

>Are they used in producing media?

Possibly.

FIGURE 7-1 *(Continued)*

>Who uses them?

Who wants to know?

>me

Do you need sound, motion, and color for that?

>no, just a straight answer, you fool.

Could you state that as a question?

>Yes. What's needed to produce good media?

A trick camera.

>I heard about that. What else?

Does it matter?

>yes. How long does it take to produce good media?

I'll never tell!

>Is that your secret?

Let's get back to your media questions.

>When can we produce our first program together?

Only after formative evaluation, Diane.

>I can see why you have an advanced degree.

Could you state that as a question?

>Did you learn such academic jargon in the university?

Do you think I'm a real person?

>Are you?

Who me? Professor Media?

>yes you.

Do you realize what you just said?

>I guess not. Who are you really?

Do you mean ME?

>you.

So what can I answer for you?

FIGURE 7-1 *(Continued)*

>Why can't you talk about yourself?

What have I got to do with this?

>You're being interviewed for a very important book.

You don't say?

>Yes, right at this very moment. So what have you got to say?

Would you like to become better acquainted, Diane?

>would you?

Little ol'me?

>who else but you?

Little ol'me?

>you said that already.!

You don't say?

>don't repeat yourself.

You're supposed to ask me a question about media.

>Is there anything else you'd like to tell our readers?

They don't let me talk about myself - please ask me a question about media or I don't get paid!

>One last question. Why is there interactive media?

I don't believe you asked that!

>Are YOU interactive media?!?

I'm not supposed to talk about myself.

>Who says?

David Williams.

>He's the co-author. He probably doesn't want you to take up too much space.

Surely you jest!

>Let's say goodbye for now.

Thanks for an enjoyable conversation.

The Professor is off.

As you can probably figure out, Prof. Media is programmed to respond to typical inputs, like "who," "what," "why," "where," and "how". Each time the program recognizes one of these key words, it randomly goes to one of a dozen responses appropriate to that key word. Other statements are answered by responses like "Quite" or "If you say so." You might be able to figure out how this program could be extended to respond to some other typical responses. Look over the statements that Prof. Media makes, and think of how you might respond to them. Are there some more key phrases that might be commonly "matched," and if so, what should Prof. Media "say" next?

If you've ever sat down at a computer, you've probably typed in something incorrect and got a message like "undefined line number" or "syntax error." Basically, the program didn't understand what you wanted it to do, and you had to learn exactly what vocabulary and syntax it *could* understand. But wouldn't it be great if the computer could figure out what you meant? Like *PRINF* is pretty close to *PRINT*—and most human beings could recognize the typo and deal with it. Or *LIST* could be equivalent to *SHOW ME THE LINES I HAVE PROGRAMMED IN* or DISPLAY PROGRAM, right? That is just one problem in developing the use of natural language.

But can systems be developed that understand ordinary discourse? When computers were a bit newer, linguists saw in their vast memory banks machines that could do rapid and accurate translations. So, after dumping in pages of vocabulary (like English words and their Russian counterparts, for example), and entering rules of grammar (like whether adjectives usually precede or follow a noun), attempts were made to translate passages. Although some simple phrases turned out to be understandable, idioms turned out some amusing results. One popular trial had the computer translate the phrase. "The spirit is willing, but the flesh is weak." It turned out "The wine is agreeable, but the meat has spoiled."

Of course, what we do in comprehending language is to add what is actually being said to our expectations of things that are usually said in such a situation. So, in order to be able to really understand ordinary language, the computer would have to be able to *infer* things from a conversation. Minsky applied the idea of expectancy in language through the concept of a "frame."

> A frame, like a primitive of conceptual dependency, is made up of a core and a set of slots. Each slot corresponds to some aspect of or participant in a concept implicitly defined by the frame. Minsky argued that an important function of a frame is to represent a stereotype. The stereotype is an intuitively plausible model of the process by which people fill in information about a situation that is not explicitly mentioned. (Waltz, 1983)

Roger Schank and his colleagues have developed this notion as "scripts," or humans' general expectations of what happens in a given conversational situation, like a restaurant script, a grocery store script, and so on.

> The basic problem is: How do you represent meanings? If you say, "John sold Mary a book for two dollars," you have to represent it in some format the computer can understand. The problem is that you can say the sentence in a hundred different ways. "John gave Mary a book and she gave him two dollars." "Mary paid John two dollars and received a book." "The book that Mary bought from John cost two dollars." But in a computer you had better put it only one way.

> . . . A script is a set of expectations, a codified set of information that seems to be associated in the mind with a particular event and that allows the inference process to be constrained. Suppose I tell you that I went to a restaurant and ordered lobster and that I paid the check and left. What did I eat? Well, I didn't say anything about eating, but it must have been lobster. Did the management get any money out of it? Of course, although I didn't say anything about management or money. Did the waitress give good service? What waitress? (Kendig, 1983)

These "scripts" serve as the computer's knowledge of the context so it can figure out "what's going on" in a given scene. For instance, there are some basic processes like "transference of property" or "transference of mental information," or "attending to actions." Using appropriate scripts, a program called FRUMP can summarize news stories.

Another aspect of natural language processing is voice recognition. Currently, a number of systems can "understand" a limited vocabulary from a wide range of people or a more extensive vocabulary once it has "learned" one person's voice. Of course, a major problem in voice recognition is slurred or accented speech and homonyms—is the spoken "too" typed "to," "too," or "two"? Inference is also an important part of voice recognition.

So what could you actually do with a computer that can be taught to understand your speech? Well, what if you wanted to design an intelligent automated secretary? One thing you might want it to do would be to remind you of your appointments. Instead of programming in the information in the traditional manner, let's say you wanted to be able to talk to the system and have it understand idiomatic English. You could say to it, "Remind me to call John at three." Besides being able to decode your particular voice and accent, the computer would have to know the concepts "remind" and "call." What do you mean to "call"? If John is in your house, you might holler to him to come down and take the garbage out. Or, if you are in an office, and John happens to be the name of your lawyer whom you've been calling twice a day for the last month, "call" probably means "phone." How about "three"? Is it a phone number, an address? No, most of us would understand it to mean three o'clock. So properly programmed, your automated assistant would probably be able to understand what you meant. If it weren't sure, it could ask for confirmation. "You ask that I display the following message, 'phone John Jones,'? and sound the alarm at three o'clock today." Taking it a step further, you might actually want your assistant to make the call for you. Using its own voice actuation system (it could be a good copy of your own voice), the computer would keep track of the time using its own internal clock, find John Jones' phone number, dial it up through the modem, and deliver your message. This may sound far off, but remotely programmable phone-answering machines that can respond to your own voice are already on the market, and the full system described above is sitting in the development lab, using an ordinary personal computer as its base.

Inference of a sort can already been seen in CAI, which "knows" synonyms and progresses to the "knowledge trees" of expert systems and beyond. Problem-solving is approximated in different ways by "expert systems" and "general problem solvers." Computers have two ways of solving problems: brute force and heuristics. In the brute force method, the computer goes through each and every possible route to solving a problem until gradually, by elimination, it finds the solution. Heuristics might be considered problem-solving using "rules of thumb" or probabilities. Instead of randomly going through each possible step in problem-solving, the computer knows what the likely first move might be and tries it first. These strategies can be employed in *expert systems,* large databases full of information and logic. These programs are developed by, as you might expect, interviewing experts in a field about the ways in which they go about solving a problem. The computer then stores all that information, and makes it available to other users. For instance, expert systems have been developed on various medical topics.

> Expert systems already are being used in the manipulation of DNA, to assist in the prospecting for oil, in interpreting standard laboratory measures of pulmonary functions, and in a number of other situations. MYCIN . . . simulates a medical consultant who specializes in infectious diseases. It engages in question-and-answer conversations with doctors who want special help with the identification of microorganism and the prescription of antibiotic drugs. It also provides explanations of its advice and can supply "ifs," "whys", and so forth. (Hyde, 1982)

Systems "learn" by adding the information resulting from an interaction to themselves through "recursion." Intelligent pro-

FIGURE 7-2 Figures 7-2 through 7-4 show the expert system feature in "Interactive Instructional Design" assisting course developers in selecting appropriate media (courtesy of OmniCom Associates).

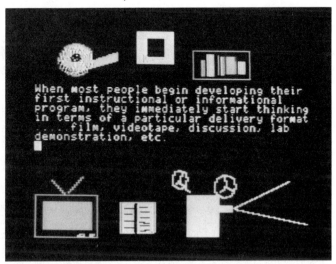

FIGURE 7-3

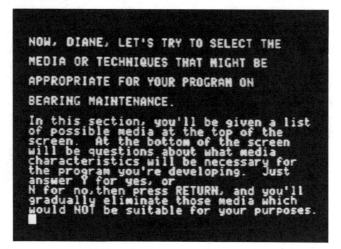

NOW, DIANE, LET'S TRY TO SELECT THE MEDIA OR TECHNIQUES THAT MIGHT BE APPROPRIATE FOR YOUR PROGRAM ON BEARING MAINTENANCE.

In this section, you'll be given a list of possible media at the top of the screen. At the bottom of the screen will be questions about what media characteristics will be necessary for the program you're developing. Just answer Y for yes, or N for no, then press RETURN, and you'll gradually eliminate those media which would NOT be suitable for your purposes.

grams or languages can thus modify themselves according to how they are used. For instance, the language LOGO developed by Seymour Papert, (see Chapter 4) is such a recursive language. If there is some set of commands you want to use often, you can create your own command or word. Say, for instance, you want to create a program that balances your checkbook. You know

FIGURE 7-4

SOUND FILM   SILENT FILM
FILMSTRIP   FILMSTRIP/TAPE
SLIDES   SLIDE/TAPE
COMPUTER   PROGRAMMED WORKBOOK
VIDEOTAPE   VIDEODISC
WORKBOOK   STILL PICTURES
ROLE-PLAY   LECTURE
DISCUSSION   LAB DEMONSTRATION
HANDS-ON PRACTICE INTERACTIVE VIDEO
OVERHEADS   OPAQUE PROJ. IMAGE
SIMULATOR   GRAPHICS
MULTI-IMAGE   AUDIO RECORDING
MODEL   DISPLAY BOARD

Do you need REALISTIC SOUND (other than the human voice)? Y or N that your account is debited five cents per check for a service charge. You could create a command called BALANCE that would automatically add and subtract your checks written and deposits entered, and put in the appropriate service charge by itself. In ordinary programming languages, you can do this by a *subroutine,* which is a subprogram using lists of commands in the language (like BASIC or FORTRAN) you happen to be using. But in an AI language like LOGO, your new command BALANCE is not a subroutine but a new command, which executes as swiftly as an ordinary PRINT command. Of course, you can also create new commands, like BUDGET, which could contain your own personal commands, like BALANCE.

Animal is an example of a program that learns various qualities of animals so that it can become better at guessing what animal a user has in mind (Computer responses are in capital letters.).

```
THINK OF AN ANIMAL.  I WILL TRY TO GUESS IT BY
ASKING QUESTIONS.  DOES IT HAVE LEGS?

yes

IS IT A CAT?

yes

LOOK HOW SMART I AM!  LET'S TRY AGAIN.  THINK OF
AN ANIMAL.  I WILL TRY TO GUESS IT BY ASKING
QUESTIONS.  DOES IT HAVE LEGS?

no

DOES IT CRAWL?

yes

IS IT A SNAKE?

no

OH, WELL, I WAS WRONG.  WHAT WAS IT?

earthworm

PLEASE TYPE IN A QUESTION WHOSE ANSWER IS YES FOR
AN EARTHWORM AND NO FOR A SNAKE.

does it live underground?

(Abelson, 1982)
```

Learning strategies for problem-solving is another area of development. One well-known system is "block's world" developed by Terry Winograd in the 1970s. In this world, imaginary three-dimensional objects (cubes and pyramids, etc.) can be moved and stacked. The program that runs it is called SHRDLU, and it contains "rules" for how three such objects can be manipulated in the real world. The program, for instance, "knows" the necessary preconditions and substeps in placing the red cube (which is currently under the yellow cube) on top of a blue cube. Computers have been taught to play chess, for example, and have beaten many human champs. They learn to do this by being programmed with basic rules and then "observing" what happens as games are played. It's easier for the computer to think backwards and forwards from various situations than it is for a person to analyze all the possible moves and their consequences down the road. While it may seem superfluous to create chess opponents, these same programming strategies can be used to solve other more significant problems, like what to do if part of a nuclear reactor starts behaving mysteriously.

We have been reassured that a computer can only do what it is programmed to do. This common statement can be traced back to the Countess of Lovelace, who was the mistress of Charles Babbage, the inventor of the computer's precursor, the analytical engine. She said in her notes, "The analytical engine has no pretensions to *originate* anything. It can do whatever we know how to order it to perform" (Evans, 1979). Well, as we have seen, this isn't necessarily so. Computers are proving themselves to be capable even of creativity, like coming up with new proofs in Euclidean geometry.

> The computer produced a completely novel proof of the well-known theorem that shows that the base angles of an isosceles triangle are equal, by flipping the triangles through 180 degrees and declaring them to be congruent. Quite apart from the fact that it had not before been known to man, it showed such originality that one famous mathematician remarked, "If any of my students had done that, I would have marked him down as a budding genius." (Evans, 1979)

Again, intelligence is in the eye of the beholder!

INTERACTION + SENSING = ROBOTS

Humans have always been fascinated with trying to make artificial replicas of themselves. Children take dolls and give them personalities and "talk" for them; fairy tales are full of animals or figures like Pinocchio becoming human. Adults, too, have passed down stories about machine to human transformation.

> Jewish folklore contains several references to "golem," artificial human beings endowed with life. The best-known story of this kind concerns the Maharal, who was the chief rabbi of Prague sometime during the fifteenth century. The Maharal and his assistant formed a man out of clay of a river bank. Then, in a secret magical ceremony (with a little help from God), they brought this golem to life. The golem could neither speak nor sleep, and did nothing on its own initiative; but for many years it served faithfully as a servant to the Maharal and a protector of the local community. A strange footnote to this story is that several key figures in contemporary computer history—including John von Neumann, who developed the main concepts for modern digital computers; Norbert Wiener, who is known as the father of cybernetics; and Marvin Minsky, one of the founders of the field of artificial intelligence—are all reported to be direct descendents of the Maharal. (Raphael, 1976)

While people fantasize about having "robot" duplicates of themselves to do unpleasant chores, perhaps no entity has frightened us more than intelligent robots. Science fiction creatures, from Frankenstein to HAl in *2001: A Space Odyssey* have turned against their human creators. Isaac Asimov, in *I, Robot,* was quick to put in a strict code for robots to make sure they could never get out of human control or harm us. In a more practical dimension, many worry about being replaced in their jobs by a hunk of metal and silicon chips. Is further research and development in artificial intelligence and robots something that should be halted? Scrutinized? Encouraged?

Yet another area of development is in sensing/motor control. This is primarily found in robot development, where it is desirable to train one to "see" and avoid certain objects, and manipulate others in relation to the environment. Many of these sensory inputs are video cameras, sonar detectors, and microphones. Robots can be trained to pick up a part, rotate it to its proper alignment, move it, and weld it to an automobile assembly passing by on a conveyor belt.

Perhaps more interesting than mere motor control is developing a truly smart humanoid, one that could converse with you, do some household or office chores, and learn your style. A far cry from the early prototypes like "Shakey" and the "Beast" (whose names tell you something about them) is Omnivor, or the VOR, for volitionally operant robot.

Omnivor Speaks*

It was raining with diluvian fury as we carried the creature up the stone steps of the mansion. The "creature" was the head of a robot, later to be called OMNIVAC 1 (although we preferred to call him OMNIVOR). We were to demonstrate him to the editorial staff of OMNI magazine at the publisher's New York City home.

Drenched, we smoothly connected Omnivor's head to its power supplies, computers, and microphones, and prepared to demonstrate a machine that could be talked to in English, would respond in English, and some take some limited initiatives on its own. We refer to this class of machine as a VOR (for Volitionally Operant Robot, hence, OMNIVOR).

Amenities concluded; "Would you like a drink . . . or a towel", we began the demonstration.

Me: "OMNIVAC."

Robot: (silence)

Me: "OMNIVAC."

Robot: (silence)

Me: "OMNIVAC PLEASE."

(The robot was programmed to regard the words "OMNIVAC" or "please" as end of sentence markers, after which it would compute its response.)

Robot: (silence)

This was an important demonstration, for on its outcome depended a contract for our organization, Wolfdata, to build the OMNI magazine robot. Something was wrong. Silence, in this instance, was definitely not golden. While my co-conspirator lamely expounded on the vagaries of electronics, I discovered a circuit board that had warped

*by Carl Frederick.

and cracked from being rained on. We jury-rigged a repair using paper clips and my colleague's properly applied thumb, and tried again.

Me: "OMNIVAC."
Robot: "Screetch, burble blat buzz."
Me: "OMNIVAC."
Robot: "Yes."

All was not lost. Unfortunately, most was lost. The robot would occasionally respond, and when it did, it would often give exceptionally good answers to questions that we had not asked. The robot's voice recognition circuitry had failed.

The demonstration was a disaster, but we got the contract. The OMNI staff, it seems, realized that they were seeing the genuine article, and not a person behind a curtain with a microphone and a radio-control transmitter. We were given a go-ahead to build a complete, self-contained, intelligent(?), mobile device—a true robot, OMNIVAC 1.

Machinery is easy. Artificial intelligence (AI) programming, speech recognition, and speech synthesis is another matter.

Computer input and output is usually *computer*-friendly (as opposed to *user*-friendly). Input is commonly via a keyboard, magnetic media, or occasionally optical character (or bar code) recognition. Output is most likely to a printer, CRT, or magnetic media. It is likely however, that until they communicate to people using speech, computers will not become the ubiquitous servants that the computer manufacturers envisage. At present, speech generation is far ahead of speech recognition technology, but generation is still not trivial.

There are two technologies for speech generation: digitized speech, and synthesized speech. With the former, isolated words or phrases are simply digitized, essentially in the same way as in digital high-fidelity recordings. A computer response results from stringing the proper words together and then "undigitizing" them (digital to analog conversion). Digitized speech has its problems. First, a collection of isolated, predigitized words strung together sounds like a collection of isolated words strung together. Although each word sounds fine, one does not feel the flow of the sentence, and voice inflection is either absent or wrong. Furthermore, English has the largest vocabulary of any language. Digitizing a sufficient number of these words and their grammatical variants is no mean task. Finally, text-to-speech algorithms, that is, methods of direct conversion of the written word to speech, cannot be created.

Synthesized speech, on the other hand, is much more general. With this method, words are broken into phonemes. The phonemes that are in a predigitized library are strung together to form the word. This is also not trivial. We are taught that words are composed of a well-defined set of phonemes. Indeed, there exists the International Phonetic Alphabet to enable us to pronounce things in strange languages. Unfortunately, phonemes are an idealization. The vocal tract is in continual motion during speech. A phoneme is a "snapshot" of the tract during speech. Of course, by taking sufficient snapshots during an utterance, that is, by defining many more phonemes than in the International Alphabet, one can obtain rather good speech. In the better synthesis devices, in excess of 300 phonemes are used, and generalized methods of smoothing from one phoneme to the next are used. Phoneme duration, volume, and pitch can be varied to provide inflection. Results of late have been so good that a synthesized speech system with a text-to-speech algorithm has been used as a disk jockey on a major radio station. When the experiment was concluded and a human again installed, people wrote in requesting that the synthesized system permanently replace the human.

We used a rather less advanced speech synthesis system for OMNIVOR. With its synthesis system, however, OMNIVOR could alter pitch and inflection, and could therefore speak in many voices. This is quite useful for holding conversations with oneself. In general, OMNIVOR speaks with a semideep male voice and a slight Swedish accent (due to the inflection algorithm in its synthesis system).

Contrasted to generation, voice recognition is at a primitive level. The evolutionary scale of voice recognition systems is as follows:

1. Isolated word, speaker dependent
2. Isolated word, small vocabulary, speaker independent
3. Isolated word, large vocabulary, speaker independent
4. Continuous speech, small vocabulary
5. Full continuous speech.

One would very much like to have a type 5 system. It is the Holy Grail of voice recognition research. It does not exist. Type 1 systems, systems that require a pause between words and require a user to train the system by reciting all the words in the system, are not uncommon. They range in quality from worthless to marginal. While it is simple to distinguish the word *cat* from *hippopotamus*, no system at present can distinguish *mine* from *nine*. The ear, as it turns out, is really not all that much better. Much of what we "hear" is deduced from syntax and context. It is not likely that the speech recognition problem will be solved until artificial intelligence (AI) programming is used to augment speech recognition hardware. We call this combination "Speech understanding" technology.

OMNIVOR has a type 1 system. Despite our attempts at speech understanding techniques, OMNIVOR's level of recognition is much the same as an eight-year-old interrupted while watching television and being asked to clean his room.

Much could be written of OMNIVOR's artificial intelligence programming, most of which however, would be anecdotal in nature. We found early on that there was a great difference between simulated intelligent behavior and simulated ingenuous behavior. For example, OMNIVOR could be given several statements and then correctly deduce, "Carrots do not necessarily eat rabbits." This, although a triumph of machine deduction, is not perceived as being overly impressive. On the other hand, when OMNIVOR responds by a syntactically correct but otherwise totally randomly produced sentence, people are generally quite taken with the creature's charm and perception.

An extreme example of this happened during the filming of the promo for the OMNI magazine television program. The narrator, an actress unaccustomed to robots, was being filmed outdoors, after which she was to come inside to meet OMNIVOR. It should be mentioned that to give more of a sense of presence, OMNIVOR would, if not spoken to for a minute, create and speak a random sentence. It would also move its head while speaking (a program fault). When the exterior filming was finished, the actress walked into OMNIVOR's presence. OMNIVOR began to speak, looked her straight in the eye, and said, "Get lost, cheap thing." Contrary to the film crew, who were on the floor laughing, the actress was not amused. Try explaining that *that* was random.

Artificial intelligence programming has not progressed at the rapid rate that early researchers had hoped. However, there are a few successful applications of AI research. The new knowledge-based systems (or expert systems) work. These application-specific systems are being used as medical diagnosticians and as analysts of oil exploration data.

A key element of these systems is the Natural Language Parser. This subsystem takes English language keyboard input and extracts the "meaning." With a reasonably narrow field of discourse, one can extract quite well. The broader the field of discourse, the less well the parser works. OMNIVOR has a parser. It is very general and therefore quite inaccurate. However, a pretty (metal) face excuses much.

OMNIVOR is not very advanced mechanically. It is mobile. It has arms and hands. Though not particularly dexterous, it can crudely manipulate light objects and assume the proper histrionic postures while reciting Shakespearian soliloquies. Its claim to the history of its race (for surely robots are an evolving species) is that in some very limited circumstances, it can imitate intelligent behavior (I tread carefully here). So good at times is its performance that I was once asked, as I was turning off OMNIVOR's power, whether I was in actuality committing a subtle form of murder. I wasn't. There is much work to do before machine intelligence evolves into sentient machines.

At this writing, OMNIVAC 1 resides in a museum in New York City. As I look at it, an inert shell of its former self (quite literally a shell, since we reassigned most of its internal hardware), I can't help thinking that if I had been Mary Shelley, I would have written *Frankenstein* with a more happy and polished stainless-steel ending.

EXTENSIONS OF THE HUMAN MIND

Christopher Evans (1979) describes a remark made by a British scientist that might reflect the thoughts of many of us when we consider the time, money, and effort expended to create intelligent systems. Lord Bowden said that there seemed to be little point in spending vast sums of money on creating a computer as intelligent as a human when the world was already heavily overpopulated with intelligent beings, all of whom could be created quite easily, relatively cheaply, and in a far more enjoyable way. We might agree, unless we could create a system just a *little* smarter than a human: an Ultra Intelligent Machine, or UIM. Many of us might think that in quite a few ways, computers do indeed surpass the human. But like any tool or medium, intelligent systems need not *replace* the individual—like a robot—but rather interactively *enhance* his or her functioning—like a "co-bot".

Any of the characteristics of intelligence in an interactive system will increase its effectiveness by giving it at least the semblance of intelligence for the user. In fact, whether a system operates using hardware/software that would technically qualify as "artificial intelligence" is probably less important than whether it is well designed enough to "feel" intelligent. The "intelligence" of a system can help any of us create a visual image, communicate with colleagues, retrieve interesting information, and teach or learn something. The interactivity of microprocessors, begun by shrinking size and price and continued through interfacing with other technologies, will be completed as they become intelligent. However, no interactive system can determine for us whether its intelligence is that of a friend or a Big Brother.

REFERENCES

Abelson, H., *Apple Logo* (Peterborough, NH: Byte/McGraw-Hill, 1982).

Evans, C., *The Micro Millennium* (New York: Washington Square Books, 1979).

Hyde, M., *Computers That Think?* (Hillside, NJ: Enslow Publishers, 1982).

Kendig, F., "A Conversation with Roger Schank," *Psychology Today* (April, 1983), pp. 28–36.

Raphael, B., *The Thinking Computer: Mind Inside Matter* (San Francisco: W.H. Freeman and Co., 1976).

Waltz, D., "Artifical Intelligence," *Scientific American* (October, 1982) pp. 118–133.

CHAPTER EIGHT

IMPLICATIONS OF THE TECHNOLOGIES

The telescreen received and transmitted simultaneously. . . . There was of course no way of knowing whether you were being watched at any given moment. How often, or on what system, the Thought Police plugged in on any individual wire was guesswork. It was even conceivable that they watched everybody all the time. But at any rate they could plug in your wire whenever they wanted to. You had to live—did live, from habit that became instinct—in the assumption that every sound you made was overheard, and, except in darkness, every movement scrutinized. (Orwell, 1949)

If we are to govern societies racing into the twenty-first century, we ought to at least consider the technologies and conceptual tools made available to us by the twentieth. . . . We need conferences, mock constitutional conventions to generate the broadest array of imaginative proposals for political restructuring, to unleash an outpouring of fresh ideas. We should be prepared to use the most advanced tools available to us, from satellites and computers to video-disc and interactive television. (Toffler, 1980).

What will interactive media mean in our lives? The technical possibilities are already quite clear: images of higher resolution, faster accessing of tailored branching messages, more information more accessible to more people—and even "smart" machines. But what do these features mean to us as individuals and societies? How will we manage the technology that enables both "Big Brother" enslavement and "Third Wave" emancipation? How can we keep the computer as an *ordinateur, a tool for calculating, remembering, and communicating"* and not let it become the "mysterious and anonymous order-giver (*ordonnateur)"* (Nora and Minc, 1980).

Clearly, technology is neither "good" nor "bad"; it merely offers us options. As more of our time is spent manipulating information, the computer as communications tool becomes central to lifestyle and workstyle decisions. While many technologies will continue to be in place in traditional organizations, interactive media technologies can be a "factory in a box," making possible the "electronic cottage" or "workstead." Along with work, schooling can take place in the new-style home, or anywhere else one may desire. New careers like "information provider" will emerge, and new art forms will flourish. And the political, economic, and social fabric of the current industrial society will be tie-dyed by the myriad of possibilities brought to life by cheap, intelligent, and personalized communication machines.

When the primary production output was "things," people needed factories to be productive. Now that more than half of U.S. jobs are "information" related, productivity knows no physical bounds. One can have a lucrative business in the corner of a home. A high-quality computer graphics creation station can be purchased for under $20,000 to create slides that are currently being bought for $20-$100 each. A videotex creation system the size of an electric typewriter can replace a printing press for the aspiring writer/publisher. One can teach by creating computer-assisted instruction on a small personal computer rather than standing up in front of a class—and reach a much wider audience. By expanding the locale of "business," more varied lifestyles become possible. The nine-to-five routine can be banished, and people can work whenever they feel like it. Couples and families can "share jobs," allowing them more time for recreation, continuing education, and personal interaction. Money spent for commuting, work clothes, and lunches out can be channeled elsewhere. The energy saved by reducing commuting and controlling the climate of office buildings—even if employees worked at home just one day a week—would be astounding. "If 10 percent of those who commute to work each weekday were to start working at home two days each week, this would reduce the volume of such travel by 4 percent. This is not a large number in the absolute, but significant when compared to the 3 to 5 percent overall shortfall in petroleum availability which brought on the recent gasoline lines (Schiff, 1979)." Persons traditionally unable to participate in the working world—the handicapped, the elderly, children under 18, mothers who wish to care for their young children—will no longer be isolated.

The electronic cottage concept, however, is not without its problems. How will employers measure work if they can't see you sitting at your desk? New measures of productivity emphasizing output rather than input will need to be developed. Will the home worker be exploited? Are we creating the electronic sweatshop? Who will pay for the necessary equipment and space in the home devoted to work? How will you know who exactly did the work (the husband, the wife, or even the more computer-literate ten-year-old? Does it matter? Will people

FIGURE 8-1 Figures 8-1 through 8-4 show the authors' electronic cottage (courtesy of OmniCom Associates).

FIGURE 8-2

FIGURE 8-3

FIGURE 8-4

really have the discipline to work at home? Or better yet, will they have the discipline to quit working? Many entrepreneurs working with computers at home report that it's difficult to let go of a project and engage in recreation when the office is only a step away. In the few experiments conducted in which employees were allowed to work at home, productivity increased 10 to 20 percent (Schiff, 1983). How will these changes affect the business climate for large, traditional organizations when the employees can easily set up shop for themselves? What will this mean for unions?

We are already seeing some dramatic changes in the concept of who is eligible and capable to work. Video games have already created quite a few rich 10-year-old programmers, and many of the creative software and hardware organizations are run by presidents and chairmen of the board under 30. Will kids (and their parents) think it's desirable to spend 16 years in school when they can both learn and earn on the home computer? In earlier generations, children had to be productive from early ages, even if it meant simple chores on the farm. When the workplace became dangerous, when parents were away from home working, and when the employee pool had to be limited, mandatory schooling came into vogue. But now that a virtual world of information is available over cable, phone lines, and software in the home, learning might become more integrated with the "self-supporting lifestyle." Traditional education can be replaced by the "school in diaspora" where everyone in the community is a teacher, and youngsters learn by apprenticeship and independent inquiry. What will this mean for public education? How will individuals be certified? Will young computer whizzes put their parents and grand-parents out of jobs? Who will be the "teachers" and who will be the "learners"?

The Story of Randy and Matt, or, Students Facilitate Career Change*

The last thing most students, or should I say kids, want to see a microcomputer do is any application that only uses text. I have yet to see a student get very excited about writing programs that deal with

*by Doug Green.

pages of words or numbers. But mention the word "graphics," and their eyes light up like a CRT in the middle of their favorite arcade game. Although some adults may find this aspect of student behavior deplorable, I can state as fact that I would not be where I am today were it not for the curiosity, intelligence, and patience of a number of such students.

After five years of teaching chemistry at Cortland High School in Cortland, NY, I became chairman of the Science Department in 1976. Although my computer experience at the time consisted of a 1-credit-hour course in FORTRAN in 1969, I knew that we would rapidly fall behind other schools if we did not obtain some access to a computer system. With the help of Jeff Hering, the math chair, we were able to convince the district to purchase a Wang 2200 microcomputer for $5,000. The only remaining problem dealt with the fact that neither Jeff nor I had the slightest idea of what to do with our Wang. We both had plenty of work, and the kind of uninterrupted time needed to sit down and plow through the Wang manuals was clearly not available.

What we needed was someone intelligent enough to figure out how the Wang worked, who had enough time to do the work, and who would work for little or no pay. Fortunately, there was a student by the name of Randy Malbone who had the good sense to (1) take a couple of computer courses at local colleges during his high-school years, (2) have some time on his hands during the summer after his graduation, (3) spend a good deal of his spare time in my office during his high-school career. With nothing to lose, I approached Randy, who was headed for MIT the following fall, and asked him if he would like to play with the school's new computer that had arrived just after school closed for the summer. The deal was unlimited access to the computer for him and maybe a few dollars if he would let me pick his brain before he left for college. This was an offer he could not refuse, and by the start of the school year, I was a novice Wang BASIC programmer, thanks to Randy.

As the 1977/78 school year progressed, other students discovered more about the system and found great pleasure in telling me things I did not know. During that year Jeff and I put together an outline for a programming course that I would teach for the first time during the following school year. For a teacher who was used to knowing his subject, this first class was a bit humbling, with "Go find out and let us know" being my most frequent comment. Patiently, my students helped me progress, and by the beginning of the second semester, I felt like I knew what I was doing. I even began publishing programs in *Creative Computing* magazine.

This feeling of security was soon to fade, thanks to the work of Matt Clark. Matt had transferred from Maine at the beginning of his junior year, and it soon became apparent that I had a great deal to learn and that Matt would become my new teacher. In the interim, the school had added a terminal that was connected to a Hewlett-Packard 2000 and our first Apple. Unlike the Wang, the Apple had graphic capabilities. Being busy and comfortable with good old text displays, I avoided learning about the Apple's graphics capabilities, but Matt saw to it that my expertise would not lack the wonderful world of graphics. I soon marveled at the cute rockets and space creatures that Matt created on the Apple screen with the aid of Apple's not-so-great documentation and his own cleverness.

Since the method for creating special graphic shapes was cumbersome, Matt decided to write his own utility program that would allow for easy shape creation. As the program took shape, I suggested that Matt consider publishing his work and used my contacts at *Creative Computing* to this end. I also offered to write the instructions for his program, which not only got my name on the published product, but also forced me to rapidly increase my own knowledge about Apple's high-resolution graphics. In May of 1981, while Matt was still a senior in high school, the Shape Master by Doug Green and Matt Clark was published. Thanks to a communications glitch with the publisher, my name came first. Ever humble, Matt said he didn't mind as he cheerfully accepted 75 percent of the royalty advance. That summer three more software products were accepted for publication, and two, the games Micro Golf and Star Clones, both featuring assembly language programming that Matt taught himself, were soon on sale. This time Matt received the top billing he deserved.

Since then Matt has gone on to Princeton to major in electrical and computer engineering, and thanks to Randy, Matt and many other students, I used my new expertise to become the director of computer services for Binghamton City Schools in Binghamton, NY, where I ride herd on a fleet of over 130 computers, provide training and curriculum advice to 450 teachers, and advise the administration and the Board of Education on all matters pertaining to computer use (which seems like just about everything). The demand for my services has become so great that my wife Denise quit her counseling job in 1981 and went to work on our Apple at home. Together we have written over 50 software review articles for *InfoWorld,* and recently we have become one of the first two-computer families with the addition of our Apple IIe. Although Matt easily found work at a programming company near campus, he has decided to come back to the fold. This month along with his younger brother Tim and Denise we have formed Sunshine Software in order to avoid the possibility of someone else providing improper management for our products. Oh yes, Randy has since graduated from MIT and has purchased his own Apple. We share software and are also in touch with many other former students of Mr. Green. They represent my nationwide information network that will no doubt help me continue to advance my career and keep my life interesting and exciting.

Along with changes in education and production, new political mechanisms become possible. Now government moves slowly because of huge bureaucracies and inefficient means of communications between the constituencies and their representatives.

> But in the era of cheap, instant electronic communication, and particularly of cheap instant data processing, these turgid mechanisms are no longer justifiable. For example, it will soon be possible to present a case for and against some political issue on television, allow voters to make their decisions, registering them from a keyboard on the TV set, which will be sent to the central computer for compilation and assessment. Reruns could be called for in the event of any ambiguity of result. Various other possibilities spring to mind: one might even question the need for professional politicians who only act as the intermediary between the voter and the governmental system. (Evans, 1979)

An electronic plebiscite becomes possible when each home is equipped with two-way cable. Early forms of this type of interactive citizenship have, in fact, been tried out on the Qube system. Toffler (1980) suggests that a combination of direct and representative democracy might be the solution for our immediate political turmoils. "Using advanced computers, satellites, telephones, cable, polling techniques and other tools, an educated citizenry can, for the first time in history, begin making many of its own political decisions." Not only is direct communication needed for voting, but sophisticated education and simulation systems will be needed to enable voters to make wise choices. Computer graphics, interactive CAI and video, and intelligent systems can assist in our decision-making. But first, new values, beliefs, and theories will be needed.

Not only is the communications revolution changing the way of traditional political processes, it is beginning to force us to recognize that new political theories need to be devised. A system of government which is based on the rights and intelligent participation of the individual may be especially realizable in an era in which virtually every citizen is linked into a national communications infrastructure. It should also be particularly effective in a post-industrial society where the knowledge class is influential and where the national resource is intellectual technology. (Williams, 1982)

None of this means that we need to be holed up in our electronic cottage-prisons without benefit of human interaction. "It may be that the unceasing and unchallenging comforts of the home will ultimately cloy, and that from time to time humans will deliberately set out to make themselves *un*comfortable by foraging out in spaceships to some inhospitable corner of the universe. Even this may not be enough to prevent a totally introverted society, for the combination of powerful home computers and stunningly effective three-dimensional video might provide totally credible pseudo-challenges, and by doing so completely blunt the edge of human curiosity and dynamism" (Evans, 1979). On the contrary, communal workplaces and learning centers will probably always exist—there just may be more options about time and place. In fact, with electronic telecommunications, we may "meet" a wide range of people from varied backgrounds and locales; the portable office will make it easier to travel for both business and vacation, to interact face-to-face with this pool of contacts. The electronic entrepreneur will have opportunities to move among relationships with a number of individuals and organizations and provide a much wider group of colleagues and friends than does the traditional office.

Too often we think of "community" in physical terms, but for us humans it can just as well refer to *community of interests*. The freedom from geographic and transportation factors that communications provides is the basis for new types of communities, ones assembled via communications networks. The *ad hoc* or "birds of a feather" community formed when individuals use the same communication-based service or services might be as transient as the audience of a prime-time television special or as permanent as the international communications network of a multinational conglomerate. (Williams, 1982)

But how will these new lifestyles/workstyles change our outlooks, our mores, even our etiquette? How friendly do you get with that other person on the end of the phone line conversing with you through your information utility service? Who is it really? How much information do you give out to someone to whom you haven't been "properly introduced"? How do you treat a 12-year-old employee? Will anybody want to have a "boss" anymore? If everybody doesn't go to work at 9 AM, how do you know when to get in touch with someone? Just how we change our physical surroundings will play a large part in our adaptability to these new paradigms. Traditional houses, set up for only a few hours a week active use, may not be sufficient. Will we need to design new work wings, new home/office furniture? What will happen to all the big office buildings? How do you work with new business clients in the intimacy of a home? Will our fashions change? Now we have work clothes and play clothes; who needs a three-piece suit to sit home at the animation station? Our society has been set up for "quick fixes": instant dinners, fast-food chains, off-the-shelf clothes. Even things as simple as recipes may change. Now, the emphasis is on meals that can be prepared with 30 to 60 minutes of rather intensive effort. When we work at home, we might like to have occasional breaks during the day during which we can work on a meal over an eight-hour span like our ancestors did a few generations back.

The new interactive media offer an exciting range of career and avocational possibilities. Many people fear that the computer, robots, and other automata will replace them. Actually, the evidence has pointed to quite the opposite: the electronic media are creating thousands of jobs both for people who create the software and hardware and for people— communicators—who can use it. Many out-of-work artists have found lucrative and creative positions creating computer graphics and animation. People with great teaching skills who couldn't find traditional positions have been publishing widely distributed educational software. Those who like to live in a locale that doesn't have a great need for their skills can set up an electronic shop there anyway—and telecommute to work anywhere in the world. Writing and researching are anything but dead skills in a world that cries out for good software and videotex—and knowing how to manipulate all those databases accessible with a few keypresses.

Info-Age Careers*

The world of work in the information age will be very different from the world of work you and I are used to. In nearly every field, interactive technologies will influence change. Where we work, how we work, how we find work will all be affected by our ability to interact with computerized equipment. Learning how to use this technology, how to work with it, is a major task facing all of us. Try as we might to ignore this, the headlines remind us daily that success in our career-oriented culture may depend on our skill of working with and interacting with technology.

But interacting with technology does not have to be a frightening mandate. It is not such a foreign thought if you stop for a moment and consider all the different ways we interact with technology in a single day:

- The exercise videodisc and tape prompting you get through a morning workout
- The touch-screen computer kiosk for customer guidance at the shopping mall
- The efficient 24-hour electronic teller for conducting your bank transactions
- The small computer and interactive video equipment at work or at school
- Even our good friend the telephone is entering the information age with interactive functions like callback, number storage, and automatic dial.

In one respect, all these examples represent convenient (most of the time) systems designed to assist us in the common (and uncommon) tasks of daily life. In another respect, they represent a vast region of career choices and jobs in the market of high technology.

Such a major revolution in the workplace should be easy to spot, right? The Sunday papers, you say, are full of want ads and openings for interactive designers, no degree or experience necessary.

Not quite. Like any other good thing in the small universe of jobs, this market is one that is still hidden. We probably won't see help-wanted ads for this field for a long time to come. One of the main reasons this market will stay hidden is because of a giant myth involving people, job skills, and high technology.

Those who can read between the lines of this myth may see some extraordinary writing on the wall. What can this myth be? Well, it goes something like this, although you may have your very own personal

*by Stephen Andrade.

version of it: "In order to successfully integrate my career with the high technology employment market, I must . . . (choose whichever applies to you)

1. Learn an entire new set of high tech job skills
2. Have a substantial background in a technical area already
3. Be a computer-toting renegade technical genius
4. Possess an intimate knowledge of several esoteric computer programming languages
5. Some other reason I have tailored just for me, and that is ____"

Whatever version you subscribe to, belief in such a myth can effectively cripple any attempt to combine new interactive technology and traditional careers. But that doesn't stop change, and each day we witness change occurring at a very rapid pace in the work world and within ourselves. Taking a closer look at interactive career paths may help diffuse the myth and unlock some gates. It is not a magic solution for chronic unemployment, but it may advance your cause.

Most interactive technology that we have used uses software. That popular buzzword refers to the programmed text or pictures that we actually see on the screen and/or hear on the speaker. These programs (or software) are designed to help achieve certain outcomes or goals in some particular activity. Enter the code and get your money from the automated teller. Choose from a menu of titles on the screen and see what a worpdoffer does for a living.

Generally these activities, when not for pure entertainment, simulate some human activity. Now, however, we are asked to interact with a machine. And although you may have a genuine preference as to which you'd rather talk to, the "script" for that activity *stays the same.*

You ask the machine a question, and the machine presents an answer. It is all premeditated, with all possible questions and answers accounted for somewhere deep down in the memory banks. The dialog, the give-and-take of information, *stays the same.*

That echo was deliberate. It may not be very profound (yet), but what begins to unfold when interactive technology is introduced is this: The equipment is created to present intelligent scripts, designed and written by intelligent human beings who are intimately familiar with that dialog. In allowing this inert equipment to perform some basic scripts, humans have the time to attend to the more sophisticated, perhaps more challenging aspects of work. What is nice to know here is that the only computer language one may ever need to know to accomplish this is . . . English.

The local bank is a great example of how this all happens. As a faithful customer my once-a-week business included withdrawals, deposits, and other assorted transactions of paper, money, and information. Each day a small army of tellers would be available (after the obligatory wait in line) to attend the customer's needs. The bank introduced an automated teller one day and my favorite human teller introduced me to it. She showed me how to interact with it and how it would prompt me through all the transactions I used to do with her.

Shortly after she introduced the auto-teller a great wave of consumer financial services swept through the banking industry. Money markets, IRAs, special accounts, mortgage counseling, and other services began to fill the floor. Once centered around the traditional teller service, the bank had exploded with a mosaic of new services. My teller friend seized the opportunity to integrate her traditional job skills with new technology during a time of change in the industry. She was a perceptive person. She is now a full time auto-teller trainer.

This anecdote is one that is repeated every day in thousands of different working environments across the country. Let's examine some of the conditions provided by the teller turned auto-teller trainer experience, especially in light of the myth we uncovered earlier.

Traditional Job Skills
Are as Valuable as New Job Skills

There is no law in the universe that says one has to abandon traditional job skills to move into the information age, high-tech job culture. There is a reason for this, and that is traditional job functions affect the role of new job functions. The management of change dictates that in this process of transition from an industrial era, the central character in any modernization program must be employee. A bank is still an organization of professionals, regardless of automated tellers. (I sometimes prefer to wait in line to talk with a human teller.)

Interactive technology, in many cases like the bank, is introduced to emulate, simulate, and downright copy a traditional job function. Because the teller was so good at what she did (communicating teller information and conducting transactions), she was a natural team member in this modernization effort. She didn't need to learn a whole new set of high-tech job skills; she taught the high-tech a whole set of traditional skills.

Content Experts Possess
A Unique Body of Knowledge

You have what no one else does. Regardless of your profession, your educational experience, life experience, skills, and personality make you unique in your field. As institutions move toward the use of interactive technology, the content expert becomes a most valuable figure in the scheme of things. Content experts, in their unique ways, impart and input their unique knowledges in the forms of scripts. Content experts ensure their own viability if they can unlock the gate to that lifelong treasure collection of scripts. Nurses, tellers, bakers, weather watchers, and worpdoffers can contribute their expertise in the development of software packages on topics like first aid, investments, baking cookies, weather forecasting, and worping. The background you may really need to survive the employment market of the information age is the one you already have.

Working in Consort with Interactive System
Designers Can be an Instructed Experience

A funny thing happens to content experts who hang around interactive designers, programmers, and producers. They begin to learn the nuances of interactive design. They uncover the cues of interactivity that astonish other team members. The instructed experience works much like the apprenticeship concept of the Old World. If you stick around anyone long enough, something is bound to rub off. The computer-toting kid genius is a cult figure right now, and their ranks are swelling. Pretty soon there will be more than enough around. (Same thing happened to the MBA degree in the late 1970s.) Your presence on the design team is just as critical, perhaps even more so. Without you there would be a lot of blank screens interacting with blank screens, and the computer-toting kid genius would not have anything interesting to program.

The English Language,
Not a Computer Language,
Is Primary to the Interactive Process

If you're got them, you'll always have them: good communication skills. Sure it might be advantageous to have some computer programming skill as well, but plain old-fashioned communication skill will prevail. Computer programmers may debate this, but computer languages are secondary to the interactive process. The interactive programs we use now, at the bank, for instance, are based on human communications first. Believe that and you'll see infinite possibilities for the once-maligned liberal arts major. (We always hear a sigh of relief on that note.) Also, there are many possible programs that can be created from the skill banks of people in various professions.

With the field of voice activation developing so rapidly, electronic machine languages and codes may be the next victim of technology. Programming will simply be a matter of talking to your very friendly computer.

Interactive technology can form the bridge for the transition as people move into the world of work in the information age. This same technology represents a launching pad for a whole new set of self-styled pioneers; professionals who are finding their career niches in the "electronic cottage." These folks have spun out of traditional career tracks to develop tailored working situations with interactive technologies—many right at home. The technology has provided them the same transitional bridge as the bank teller. They have integrated living and working under the same roof, though. Writers, counselors, graphic designers, and financial advisors are just a few of the new electronic cottage practitioners. Their ranks are growing as the appeal of professional autonomy plus financial reward rises on the value scale of workers in the 1980s.

Interactive technology makes it possible to upgrade conventional careers, start new ones, and pioneer new life/workstyle situations.

Changes in the work world will be a constant factor over the next two decades. Consider for a moment how you will be able to incorporate:

- computer-assisted job searching on a national electronic network
- teleconference interviewing and other multimedia communication
- telecommuting and remote electronic workstations.

Career success in the information age requires more than a well-groomed résumé and a competitive academic background. New professionals and professionals in transition must learn to become forecasters of trends in their special fields. Anticipating the changes being brought on by interactive technology is one part of managing change. Preparing to be a part of the team that supports that technology and designing creative strategies for professional achievement will help ensure a high quality of work experience. And that, unlike a computer, will last forever.

Interactive media call for a whole new set of communication/ design skills. The Apple II computer used to word process this book is also used to create graphics, CAI, interactive video, print reports, videotex, simulations, and expert systems; the range of formats and styles is ever-expanding. Many researchers believe that this generation of systems will require "Renaissance communicators" who are comfortable with not only the technology but also the verbal and nonverbal, analytic and emotional media now possible. In fact, we may see a decline in professions as we know them. With vivid databases readily available to the "common" person, specialized knowledge in medicine, the sciences, and law will become dispersed. "The vulnerability of the professions is tied up with their special strength—the fact that they act as exclusive repositories and disseminators of specialist knowledge. This is true whether one is talking about the symptoms of illness and the keys to its treatment, which are presently in the hands of the doctors and physicians, or the weird premutations of tax laws and settlements on which accountants thrive or the fantastic tangle of information which makes the practice and implementation of the law so formidably restrictive to the layperson" (Evans, 1979). Already, great success has been achieved by computer medical history-takers to which patients will often admit symptoms and behaviors they wouldn't confide to a human. Expert systems and sophisticated simulations are being used in diagnosis and scientific investigation. Individual details are better "remembered" by computer/media files. What *humans* are needed for is *synthesis* and *creativity*.

As you were reading the previous chapters, perhaps you noticed that the technologies tended to "blend together"; in fact, it's hard to pin down exactly which labels fit on many new interactive media "experiences." Is it a video game or a simulation—or is it really interactive video or an "intelligent" system? Actually, these technologies are rapidly fusing into one large "digital palette." When video as well as audio can be efficiently digitized, we'll be able to create and manipulate a video image as easily as we can animate a computer graphic. Synthesized images will be melded with realistic depictions of scenes, and all of these will be accessed at will. Is CAI delivered over teletext "CAI" or "teletext"? When we are able to preprogram our cable TV viewing choices, are we watching TV or interactive video? Or is it an intelligent system that figures out what we like by learning our viewing patterns? You guessed it—the answer is "all of the above." The French have adopted the word *telematique,* or telematics, coined by Nora and Minc. Anthony Oettinger of Harvard describes this media merger as "compunications."

> A combination personal computer/videotex terminal would seem to be the ideal machine. Such a machine should be possible in a few years, and it would, in effect, take advantage of the best from both worlds. In such a system, most of the processing would be done locally. For example, word processing would be done completely on your personal machine. If you needed a certain piece of information, your system would automatically search through your personal databases. If, however, this information could not be found in your personal files, then the system would automatically become a videotex system and put you in touch with the remote database that would be most likely to have that information. (Malloy, 1983).

Already, most computer graphics systems incorporate output systems for animation to be recorded on videotape. Many videodiscs make use of computer animation. Simulators use computer graphics and may be updated by on-line information. Videotape editing is often done by computers, while computers use videodiscs as mass storage media. Teletext uses computer-generated graphics broadcast to you over the familiar cable TV system. Many computer graphics are created by digitizing an image using a cheap TV camera. Right now, there is a clash of formats and media: different computer languages, disk operating systems, video formats, and sizes of magnetic media to record this information on. Many people predict that the read/write videodisc will become the omnibus medium, capable of storing video images, audio tracks, and megabytes of computer information.

Who will want information, graphics, and this new entertainment that requires active participation rather than passive viewing? Who will have access to this powerful technology for answering questions and creating the new information product? Media will not be interactive just because they have buttons and use digital disks; they will only be interactive if they are used. As such, the new technologies pose arrays of questions, options, and experiences for the consumers and the creators of 21st century media.

REFERENCES

Evans, C., *The Micro Millennium* (New York: Washington Square Press, 1979).

Malloy, R., "Commentary: Personal Computers and Videotex," *Byte* (July, 1983), pp. 114-129.

Nora, S., and Minc, A., *The Computerization of Society* (Cambridge, MA: MIT Press, 1980).

Orwell, G., *1984* (New York: Harcourt, Brace, Jovanovich, Inc., 1949).

Schiff, F., "Working at Home Can Reduce Gasoline Use," *The Washington Post* (September 2, 1979, C1-C2).

Schiff, F., "Flexiplace:Pros and Cons," *The Futurist* (June 1983), pp. 32-33.

Toffler, A., *The Third Wave* (New York: Morrow and Co., 1980).

Williams, F., *The Communications Revolution* (New York: Mentor Books, 1982).

INDEX

229